Moving Mountains is not your ordinary story of survival. This is an account of true miracles and the strongest bond of love between husband and wife I have ever encountered. Whatever phase of life in which you are currently, even if you feel your spiritual growth and faith is strong and solid, do yourself a favor and not just read this book, EXPERIENCE this book. I can comfortably guarantee two things, 1) When you reach the last page of their story you will want more, and 2) You will be moved to love more, trust more, and understand a God who "has your back."

Jo Ludwig, RPh, MA, LPC
Racine Dominican Associate

The healing power of the Holy Spirit flows through every step of Jan and Michael Burroughs' journey of divine love and compassionate grace. The details chronicled in *Moving Mountains* transport the reader into the realities and aftermath of unexpected tragedy, painstaking surgical procedures, focused rehabilitation, human error, spiritual crisis, surrender of dreams, faithful acceptance, gratitude for each moment, and eternal love. Their unforeseen pilgrimage through the aftermath of a terrible car crash and three strokes has touched hundreds, and soon to be thousands, of lives as family, friends, communities, healthcare providers, and readers of this amazing book witness in awe the dedication, compassion, resilience and unconditional love between these two souls; a reminder to all that God's love flows through each of us offering comfort, peace, and healing in ways not necessarily visible with the eyes yet clearly visible with our hearts.

Amy Camie, CCM
Certified Clinical Musician and Professional Harpist

Author of *Loving Life...All of it—A Walk with Cancer, Compassion, and Consciousness*

Skip the soaps...read this book to get a glimpse of what a real marriage can be. Don't uncap the Coca Cola...instead toast Jan and Michael Burroughs and their friends with some age-old wine for a taste of the real deal. You will not be sad when you finish this book. But what a real marriage might cost you will hit you between the heart and soul. We need doses of reality like this one. It's a quite a ride. Read this book!

Carla Mae Streeter, OP
Professor Emerita
Systematic Theology and Spirituality
Aquinas Institute of Theology

Moving Mountains is an easy and inspiring book to read. The reader will experience just a small portion of the ordeal the author, Michael Burroughs, and his wife, Jan, underwent after a terrible car crash that severely injured her, resulting in many months of grueling therapy, and the three strokes she suffered during the following year. The sustaining thread in their experiences is that a seemingly small 'mustard seed of faith' accomplishes far more than they or we might ask or imagine. As the title suggests, in this powerful story, faith and hope abound, and small seen miracles and large unseen miracles both become apparent. This book has helped me in some recovery of my own regarding a seriously ill loved one. Through his writing Michael has also provided 'spiritual direction' to me. He also gives sound advice on crisis planning and actions one should take as a caregiver in the face of strokes.

The Reverend Wilson Nathaniel Pyron, Jr.
Priest Retired
The Episcopal Diocese of Missouri

In *Moving Mountains*, Brother Michael Burroughs has written an important book. It is important as a practical guide for those caring for loved ones who have suffered strokes. It also offers an important study of the Christian work of pastoral care, which Jesus directed us all to practice. It provides us with a valuable spiritual autobiography of "faith under stress," a faith tested in the fire of heartbreaking challenges. But most importantly, Brother Michael enriches us with a love story, a story of the struggle he and his wife continue to endure. Here we encounter a remarkable truth: there is no Christian story that does not have, at its core, a love story.

James R. Dennis, OP
Master, Anglican Order of Preachers (Dominican)

Life is hard, but sometimes things hit so hard one struggles to make sense of it all. It is when that burden becomes so heavy we ask: "What do I do?" "Where do I go for answers? "How can I continue?" Michael Burroughs, the author of this inspiring book, *Moving Mountains*, has done a masterful job describing the mountain he and his wife, Jan, encountered following a life threatening car crash that injured her severely, and three subsequent strokes she suffered during the next year. Even more, he reveals how his faith in God and the power of the Holy Spirit has made all the difference in his journey of life and love. God has given us power to stand, endure, and overcome our circumstances; but learning how to harness that power is often never understood, much less realized. Michael is harnessing that power for his beloved wife. For all those who struggle with such a burden as theirs, you will be blessed in reading this book. It will enlighten, strengthen, and encourage you.

James T. Patterson, PhD
Colonel, USAFR (Ret)
Author of *Bleeding Out In the Pews*

Moving Mountains is an odyssey of discovering the miracle of faith. This book is a valuable journal for every family and caregiver of a stroke patient, as well as anyone facing a personal life and death crisis. It documents in detail the many valuable lessons Jan and Michael Burroughs learned during the moments of tragedy, fear, and hope—lessons that can only be resolved with determination, persistence, love, and unyielding faith in the healing power of the Holy Spirit. It exemplifies the truth of the power of belief, which can only be revealed to you when you surrender all and accept that the miracle of healing is spiritually possible and real. The loving compassion and total commitment that Michael details and shares in this book profoundly demonstrates how his faith, hope, and love provides many experiences that are valuable lessons for anyone who reads this amazing story. It is an odyssey of their unbreakable bond of love, and miracles only obtainable through faith and confident expectations.

John Camie
President
Blue Star Productions, Inc.

This book is first of all a love story. I have been privileged to know and minister to the author, Michael Burroughs, and his remarkable wife, Jan, since she suffered her first of three strokes. Their love for each other is extraordinary. This powerful book, *Moving Mountains*, takes you through each of their life altering crises: a horrendous car crash that crippled his wife for a year, and the three subsequent strokes she suffered the following year. The journey he takes you on runs the gamut of emotions from shock, to fear, to despair, to faith and hope. It describes how he has learned to rely on the Holy Spirit for her healing and the many lessons he has learned along the journey. In the midst of her recovery I was blessed to conduct a wedding vow renewal ceremony on their 50th anniversary, which touched me deeply. It is an inspiring story and is a book you will likely want to share with others, especially caregivers, in search of a pathway through a life-altering physical and spiritual crisis.

The Reverend Thomas Albinson
Episcopal Priest and Assistant Rector

The Church of St. Michael and St. George

In this soulful book, *Moving Mountains*, Michael Burroughs shares a deeply personal journey of love, caring, self-giving, and faith, in facing a life changing situation full of uncertainty—the devastating experience of his spouse who was severely injured in a car crash, and was in the hospital and rehab for an entire year, only to be felled by three strokes in the first half of the following year resulting in impaired memory and speech as well as immobility. Michael and his wife, Jan, have clearly placed themselves in the hands of God. The deep and abiding love which this couple shares for each other is abundantly apparent throughout the pages of this book, as they inspire many others along their journey. Their shared experience will be a soul enriching read, and especially inspiring for anyone whom life has placed in the position of such loss and being a caregiver for a loved one.

Br. Franklin Kline, OP
Anglican Order of Preachers (Dominican)

MOVING MOUNTAINS

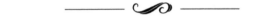

Facing Strokes with Faith and Hope

Michael K. Burroughs

XULON PRESS

Xulon Press
2301 Lucien Way #415
Maitland, FL 32751
407.339.4217
www.xulonpress.com

Moving Mountains: Facing Strokes with Faith and Hope
© 2020 by Michael K. Burroughs

Unless otherwise indicated, Scripture quotations taken from the
Holy Bible, New International Version (NIV). Copyright © 1973,
1978, 1984, 2011 by Biblica, Inc.™. Used by permission. All rights
reserved.

Burroughs, Michael K., 1950 –

Printed in the United States of America.

Paperback ISBN-13: 978-1-6312-9683-3
eBook ISBN-13: 978-1-6312-9684-0

I dedicate this book to the love of my life, Jan Burroughs, whose two-year recovery through a series of debilitating injuries and strokes has inspired me and all who know her. I'm so blessed to have been married to her, this remarkable woman, for the past 50 years. What an amazing life we have lived!

Jan Burroughs, Venice, Italy

I tell you the truth. If you have faith the size of
a mustard seed, you will say to this mountain,
"Move from here to there," and it will move.
Nothing will be impossible to you.
    Matthew 17:20 NIV

And these signs will accompany those who believe: In my
name they will drive out demons; they will speak in new
tongues;...they will place their hands on sick people and
they will get well.
    Mark 16: 17,18 NIV

Is any one of you sick? He should call the elders of the
church to pray over him and anoint him with oil in the
name of the Lord. And the prayer offered in faith will
make the sick person well. The Lord will raise him up.
    James 5:14,15 NIV

Now faith is being sure of what we hope for
and certain of what we do not see.
    Hebrews 11:1 NIV

If you believe, you will receive whatever you ask for.
    Matthew 21:22 NIV

Do not be anxious about anything, but in everything, by
prayer and petition, with thanksgiving, present your
requests to God, and the peace of God which transcends
all understanding, will guard your hearts and minds in Christ Jesus.
    Philippians 4: 6,7 NIV

Everything is possible for him who believes.
    Mark 9:23 NIV

TABLE OF CONTENTS

ACKNOWLEDGEMENTS

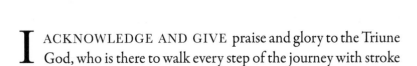

I ACKNOWLEDGE AND GIVE praise and glory to the Triune God, who is there to walk every step of the journey with stroke patients and their care partners. Miracles do happen.

I am grateful and abounding with love for my sons, Michael Jr. and John, who have encouraged me from the first day of my care partner journey, knowing that their mother is in the best hands possible. They have also urged me to write this book and tell this story as I negotiate the challenges of her care and the details of the experience and the lessons learned while all are still clear in my mind.

We owe a great debt to our many friends and family: Jo and Ken Ludwig, Amy and John Camie, Bev and Fred Miller, Ginger and Gary Johnson, Gloria and Doug Campion, Lori and Dick Moore, Carla Mae Streeter, Miranda Metheny, Margaret Chance, Randy Chance, Matthew Potter, Alex Lindley, Donna Mertz, Bettilynn Ford, Jim Patterson, Nathaniel Pyron, Ophelia Wilson, Carole Sanford, Mare Wheeler, Elizabeth, Mary, and Janie (healers from The Shepherd's Table) and so many others who have been there for us when we have needed them most.

We are forever indebted to the hundreds of people who actively pray for us, namely: The Racine Dominican Sisters, the

Racine Dominican Associates, the Anglican Order of Preachers (Dominican), the Goodlettsville High School Class of 1968, the Madison High School Class of 1968, The Board of Directors of Project Wake-up, the healing ministers of The Shepherd's Table and Catholic Charismatic Renewal, The adult Sunday school class of the Long Hollow Baptist Church, Higher Ground Holiness Church, The Church of St. Michael and St. George, John G. Lake Ministries, PEO, Andrew Wommack Ministries, the American Association of University Women (AAUW), Unveiled Life Power School Pillar 1 Student Group, Sister Carla Mae Streeter, The Reverend Wilson Nathaniel Pyron, Jr., The Reverend Tom Albinson, Bridget Schaefer, Karin Bohn, Denny Taylor, Janet Nimer, Sister Karen Vollmer, Sister Ruthanne Reed, Colonel Jim Patterson, Mare Wheeler, Denny Lind, Pastor Wayne Winchester, Elizabeth Barbieri, Beverly Williams Stypula, Gloria Horton, Steve Smith, Rosalyn Heath Sprinkles, and many others known and unknown.

I am grateful to the staff of Mercy Therapy Services, Town and Country, Missouri, who were dedicated to rehabilitating Jan following two hospitalizations—after our wreck, and her first stroke.

The Reverend Tom Albinson, Episcopal priest, assistant rector of the Church of St. Michael and St. George, has been by our side through Jan's strokes and officiated at our vow renewal ceremony on our 50th wedding anniversary.

The Reverend Wilson Nathaniel Pyron, Jr., retired Episcopal priest, has been a spiritual rock for us and has been by our side through Jan's strokes. He has been our friend for over twenty years and has been a counselor and spiritual director to me throughout this journey.

I am grateful for the direct healing ministry to Jan and me by Bob Spurlock, Bob Lindquist, Rick Turner, Jim Holtom, Gary

Jepsen, Tony Myers, and indirectly through their healing ministries by Millian Quinteros, Andrew Wommack, Elisha Randle, Jeff Randle, Curry Blake, Tom Loud and Pete Cabrera, Jr., who travel the nation and the world for God as they heal the sick, perform miracles, and make disciples.

FOREWORD

———— ◦◞◦ ————

Y ES IT'S TRUE. You don't give a testimonial without first having gone through a test. What you are about to read is both. It is a testimonial, but you can't miss it...it is indeed a test.

We all come up against our 'mountains.' Many of us try to figure how to go around them. Some of us just get paralyzed and sit down immobile before them. But cast that mountain into the sea? That takes something else. We need real life examples of tough faith to challenge us to go this route.

You have such an example in this book. As you read you will be saddened, grieved, depressed, amazed and inspired. Get ready for the ride.

Michael Burroughs is not going to paint the usual soap opera rendition of a marriage relationship for you. He is going to show you how, through faith he has experienced a mountain casting itself into the sea as he lives his marriage commitment. No one is more astonished at what he writes than he is. His telling of the story is not maudlin or whiney, not full of self-pity or depression. He will tell you what happened with a cool directness and with carefully checked-out facts. Then he will invite you to sit next to him as the mountain uproots itself and plunges into that Sea-Mystery that surrounds all of us as we daily live our little lives.

As an associate of a women's religious community dedicated to the Catholic mystic, Catherine of Siena, Michael is familiar with one of her famous images. Catherine took a boat trip on the Mediterranean one day. When she returned, she wrote her Dominican 'watch-dog' Raymond of Capua (The Dominicans assigned him to accompany her, because they feared she might embarrass them.). She wrote that she was amazed at how wide and expansive the sea was. Then, she said, she went to pray, and God said to her, "Catherine, I am the Sea, the great Sea of Peace; and you, Catherine, are the fish." With this simple statement, Catherine forever gained the insight into the proportion needed for a proper relationship with this Mystery by faith.

Michael Burroughs will make a similar discovery as you read these pages. He will begin in Part I by introducing you to the love of his life, Jan. Then you will watch in horror as their lives are turned upside down. You will watch Michael, as a fish, flounder about... questioning everything and understanding little. Yet even here, in this early part of their story, you will sense that he is not drowning. He may be gasping for breath, but he is not drowning.

Part II, Part III, and then Part IV will take you into still deeper water. As you read, I suggest you keep alert for the mountain beginning to move. It's in between the lines...watch for it. By the end of Part IV Jan will be at home and Michael will be transformed. The mountain has indeed cast itself into the Sea, and there is a Golden anniversary celebration of 50 years of marriage. But the story doesn't end there. Michael tries to explain what has happened to him these past two years, and in Part V we will witness how he explains what has happened to him.

It is in this final section that Michael renders us a real service. These final pages are not just laying out his faith journey, rich as that is. They are chock full of very practical advice and concrete suggestions for any of us who go through a serious illness as a caregiver, specifically with a stroke patient. There is a mountain of Medicare forms that cover his dining room table. There is advice about such things as a Power of Attorney, and much more. If you are struggling with a loved one who has suffered a stroke, or other debilitating illness or injury, take notes! The practical advice will serve you well.

The book closes where Michael has taken us. Jan remains at home under his daily care. She is at peace in his love, and at this writing, she is healing and there have been no further strokes. Think what you may, this may be the wonderful result of how his love feeds her heart, and continues to heal her body, with a little help from macha green tea, her attendant, Ophelia's, tender and upbeat care, and a tremendous amount of healing prayer from a lot of folks. And Michael? He tells it like it is for him. He is taking one day at a time.

Carla Mae Streeter, OP
Professor Emerita
Systematic Theology and Spirituality
Aquinas Institute of Theology
St. Louis

PREFACE

N HIS BOOK, *Overcomer*, Dr. David Jeremiah, prolific spiritual author and pastor, tells us that you can't have a testimony
without first having a test. Our test began on January 26, 2018, when
my wife, Jan, and I were barely spared death when an errant teenager
hit our car doing 80 mph on a residential road, and through three
hemorrhagic strokes that struck her during the first half of 2019. It
continued through her long road to recovery while in the hospital
multiple times, in rehabilitation, and recovering at home.

This book is the beginning of our testimony. It is a faith journey.
I will be going into this in much detail in the following pages. Suffice
it to say this has been the most profoundly spiritual challenge I have
ever encountered. It has also been the basis for spiritual growth like
I never imagined. I know myself well, and I am certain that were
God not continually by our sides, this story would be quite different.

It was well after her first stroke it was confirmed Jan had an
incurable and untreatable brain disease called, Cerebral Amyloid
Angiopathy (CAA). It is a rare condition in which a toxic protein
(beta amyloid) creates plaque in the small and medium-sized vessels
of the brain and erodes the vessel integrity resulting in spontaneous
hemorrhages.

Jan's first stroke on February 28th 2019 was in her right temporal lobe. She was still able to walk and talk, but she suffered a significant loss to her short term memory, her cognition was also affected, and she experienced behavioral symptoms that further complicated her condition.

Her second stroke occurred on June 6th 2019 and affected her left temporal lobe and other areas of her left hemisphere. This resulted primarily in her speech and language processing center being severely impacted along with further degrading of cognition. The result was a condition known as Aphasia, which affects her language receptivity as well as her speech. In her case she has "global aphasia" this condition results in speech that is a combination of normal words and short sentences intermixed with gibberish ("word salad"). Often it is as difficult for them to receive spoken communication as it is to speak it, and it impacts reading and writing. This stroke also affected her mobility somewhat.

Her third stroke occurred on July 17th 2019 while she was in rehab for her second stroke. It was actually in three locations: her motor cortex on the right hemispheric side, her right frontal lobe, and somewhat in her left frontal lobe. This stroke created spasticity in her left leg and arm and made it impossible for her to stand. Her executive functioning was also impacted, which further impaired her ability to reason and communicate.

During her third hospitalization, her neurologist and neurosurgeon informed me that there was nothing more they could do for her and recommended I take her home and "make her comfortable." Since July 27th 2019 she has been at home confined to a hospital bed we have installed in our den, and also in a wheelchair. We have 24/7 caregiver support. These two ladies live with us: one for four days straight, and the other one for three days straight. They take good care of bathing, grooming, dressing, feeding, interacting, and moving Jan from her bed to her wheelchair and, from there, around the house, as appropriate. She takes her breakfast in bed and her lunch and dinner meals from her wheelchair at the kitchen table. Her appetite is very good, as are her vital signs. Her disposition is surprisingly good. Her wonderful personality shines through all the time.

When Jan came home she was placed in "palliative care" and is managed through the Visiting Nurse Association's Advanced Illness Management (AIM) program. Their goal is to keep her well cared for and out of the hospital unless absolutely necessary. In addition to AIM, she has two primary care physicians and two nurse practitioners who care for her at home, when necessary.

When she had her first stroke I was still working part time as an executive coach. Due to her relatively stable condition, I was able to continue working. After her second stroke, that changed. I could not be depended upon to meet my client appointments and obligations and decided that I could no longer be both a full time caregiver and a working professional, so I officially retired. I have no regrets. God has blessed us with Jan's teacher's pension, my pension as a retired Army colonel, my social security, and some income from a variety of other sources, so I did not have the financial pressure to continue to work and could devote my full time and attention to her.

Healthcare coverage has also been a blessing. In 2015, we both went on Medicare. My being retired from the military, we are also covered by Tricare, the military's healthcare insurance available to military retirees.

A situation we have had to get used to has been the presence of other people in our house around the clock. At first, that was stressful, as it was a new experience, and I had to ensure my support team consisted of the right people. We are blessed with a good home care company and I was able to narrow the field down to two excellent caregivers. Home attendant care is a huge expense, and it is all coming out of our monthly income and nest egg. We were unable to get long term care insurance years ago due to our both having pre-existing conditions.

I've spent the past year researching everything I possibly can about her condition—the nature of her strokes, the causes, her prognosis, and her medications. It has helped me immensely when dealing with healthcare providers to be able to communicate with them on a fact-based level.

This book's title is, *Moving Mountains*. It comes from Matthew 17:20. Jesus is chastising some of his disciples who are perplexed that they have been unable to cast out a demon like Jesus does. He tells them they are unable to do so because they lack sufficient faith, saying that if they had faith as small as a tiny mustard seed they could command a mountain to "move from here to there" and it would obey them. Jesus says that with sufficient faith there is nothing that would be impossible to them. I have faith. I've had it for as long as I can remember. I've never measured the size of it. I don't need to move a physical mountain. Jan's healing is my mountain. It requires a belief that it can be done, faith enough to pray (and obtain prayers from others) for her divine healing, hope sufficient to create the expectation that she will eventually recover, and persistence to keep at it until she does. The Apostle Paul says *Faith is being sure of what we hope for and certain of what we do not see.* Hebrews 11:1 NIV.

In the book, *The Miracle Ship*, by Brian O'Hare, John Gillespie, the well-known Irish healer, says God's expectation in healing prayer is that we "...call things into being that have not yet happened, as though they will happen, until they do happen." He also says that healing is not always for the present, sometimes it is for the future. The Catholic evangelist and healer, Eddie Russell, in his book, *12*

Steps to Divine Healing, says we must be specific about what we ask for and we must believe we will receive exactly that. I call it, "blessed assurance."

Do I get anxious about the mountain facing us? Absolutely! But I draw comfort daily in Paul's exhortation to the Church in Philippi on the subject of anxiety. He says, *"Don't be anxious about anything, but in everything, by prayer and petition, with thanksgiving, present your requests to God, and the peace of God which transcends all understanding, will guard your hearts and your minds through Christ Jesus."* Philippians 4:6,7 NIV. I am rarely anxious these days and am at peace. I recite this verse to myself most days.

Along this journey I have encountered many people who have a demonstrable indwelling of the Holy Spirit. These people have changed my outlook on healing. Having been baptized in the Holy Spirit is what has propelled Jan and me through our lives together and this journey. We have had faith all along that whatever God chooses for us, we are ready. We pray, as do so many others, the outcome will be her recovery, and once that occurs, she will be an active testimonial to others as to the healing power of the Holy Spirit.

There are tens of thousands of Spirit-filled people who go about healing ministries every day, in every corner of the world. Prophetically, on three occasions in the months leading up to Jan's second stroke when she lost her voice, she told me she believed that I was a healer and needed to pursue that calling. I have since had others tell me the same thing. We often learn of our spiritual gifts through people who are given the prophetic voice to tell us what they are. It's no coincidence that I first heard this from Jan. I'm following her lead and am being mentored and supported by several divine healers who practice that spiritual gift on a global scale.

In the following pages I share our experiences in 2018, 2019, and 2020, beginning with the horrendous car crash we experienced (and barely survived) in January of 2018. I start there because the aftermath of that wreck, and Jan's year of recovery, has had a direct impact on her subsequent stroke history. Following that, I recount the experiences of each of her strokes in the first half of 2019, and our ongoing life of faith, therapy, and daily care, since then. I end our story recounting the amazing spiritual journey we have been on from the beginning of our ordeal—and even in the months before the wreck leading up to that pivotal date. And finally, I share numerous lessons I have learned along the journey these past two and a half years in hopes they can help other stroke patient caregivers better negotiate the healthcare system and the world of divine healing.

May you be blessed, encouraged, and informed by taking this journey with us.

Michael K. Burroughs
August, 2020
St. Louis, Missouri

Part I

——— ❧ ———

THE WRECK

Chapter 1

Our Worst Day

---⸙---

THIS IS A book about a faith journey through the world of strokes. The wreck we barely survived had a direct impact on Jan's subsequent strokes. It's pivotal to our journey. So I begin with it.

Friday, January 26, 2018, was a nice day. The sun was shining, and, while chilly, we did not need to wear our heavy coats we had brought with us for a typical January day.

Most Fridays, the Assumption Greek Orthodox Church, in Town and Country, Missouri, serves a scrumptious Greek lunch to the public. The staff is all volunteers from the church, and the food is so good, people flock to them every week. Their dining room is the gym and auditorium for the Greek school that is co-located with the church. It is full every Friday. The menu is published monthly and, depending on the menu, there can be so many people that they sell out. The most popular meal is a lamb shank, but everything they serve is excellent. Every Friday they serve a baked white fish with a vegetable that is the best I have ever eaten, anywhere. Jan and I have eaten at this church about 30 times per year. Usually we have the fish. They serve from 11 to 2, so it's important to get there on time. That day it was especially important that we do so.

On January the 26th we were heading to lunch and running a little bit behind. We live about eight miles from the church. That day I had a client meeting at 3:30, so we would need to make the trip, eat, return home to let Jan off, and then I would retrace my steps and add about three miles to get to where my executive coaching client would be expecting me. To save time (due to the heavy traffic on our normal route to the church) I decided to go the "back way," down a residential four lane road near our home. I figured we would save 10 to 15 minutes by going that way. It was a fateful decision I have mulled over numerous times since then. I wish to God I had not done it.

As we were driving in the left hand east-bound lane, Jan was all smiles and telling me how good she felt and how much she loved being out on such a nice day. We were in the middle of a pleasant conversation and were only about a mile and a half from our home as I was topping a gentle rise doing the speed limit (40 mph). There was a car in front of us about two hundred feet ahead, and a car in the right hand lane about one hundred feet in front of us. In mid-sentence, we were suddenly hit hard on the passenger door and right front fender. The impact sent us spinning across the turning lane and two oncoming lanes of traffic. Miraculously, the oncoming traffic avoided hitting our spinning car. Once across the two lanes, we hit a curb head on and about eight feet later hit a decorative stone retaining wall head on. All six airbags were inflated. The breath was knocked out of both of us and the car was filling with smoke. I thought immediately that I had broken both wrists and my left knee (but had not). My chest was in a lot of pain due to the seat belt grabbing me at that speed. And my back hurt. In the following seconds I had no idea what had happened (I had not seen the car that hit us) and I did not know how severely Jan was hurt.

Let me say, before getting too far into our story that being hit by a car doing 80 mph is a horrific experience. The violence is indescribable. If a wreck like ours has never happened to you thank God for it and pray it never does. If it, or something similar, has happened to you, chances are you not only thank God you survived, but pray every time you have gotten into a car since then that nothing like that ever happens to you again.

After we hit the wall we both started yelling for help. There was no need. Within about two minutes there were several people on each side of our wrecked car. My window still operated and they said to hold on, the police and ambulance had been called and were on the way. The smoke filled car was due to all six of the airbags exploding; we were not on fire as we had feared. Soon the police and the paramedics arrived and went to work.

I was able after a few minutes to climb out of the car. Jan was unable to do so. As the police and paramedics were questioning me, I saw two paramedics attempting to remove Jan from her seat. She screamed in pain. I could see clearly her right ankle was badly broken. I assumed there were more, possibly worse, injuries. The car that hit us impacted right where she was sitting.

I remember getting very irritated that the police and paramedics who were on my side of the car seemed only interested in paperwork: my license, my proof of insurance, and my medical insurance cards (we are on Medicare with a Tricare supplement). As Jan was being carried to the ambulance on a gurney, the medics wanted to see her medical insurance cards, too. Her purse had been knocked into the very back of our 2016 Honda CRV along with my mobile phone and glasses. While I'm desperately trying to get to Jan, the paramedics on my side of the car continued their pursuit of proper documentation. Though unsaid, it was clear to me they wanted to know who would be paying for the ambulance ride. There was an ambulance for me, as well. I told them, no, that I would be riding with Jan in her ambulance. They said I could if I insisted, but I would need to ride in the front passenger seat. With all of our personal belongs and coats and hats, I managed to get to her ambulance just before they left for the hospital.

The ambulance was en-route to the hospital, a Level 1 trauma center about eight miles away. It was the closest Level 1 trauma center to the scene of the wreck. It was a logical place to go. On the way to the hospital I called the company I was working for to briefly tell them that 1) we had been in a terrible crash, 2) I would be missing my appointment scheduled for about three hours later, and, 3) they would need to reassign my other seven clients to other executive coaches. There was no doubt in my mind I would not be working as a coach anytime soon.

On the way to the hospital, I prayed to God he would spare Jan. I didn't know the extent of her injuries, so was very anxious. I knew our lives had forever changed in a moment. While not knowing how it would manifest, I knew the future did not bode well for us. Everything was now different—a new course was being charted, but it was being charted into the unknown, the abyss. I was frightened and simply pleaded with God that he would not leave her side and would see her through the ordeal in front of her. I prayed also that whatever she faced, I would be up for the task as well. She was going to have to rely on me in ways she had never done before. Jan is fiercely independent. That worldview was now fading behind her as we ventured into the unknown. I was unsure of what exactly would be required of me, assuming she survived the next few days, but I knew I would need to be the best possible husband, advocate, support system and caregiver. As daunting as the task appeared on the front end, I still underestimated it by a wide margin. I found myself praying all the time, a veritable running dialogue with the Lord. The theme was always the same: save her, help me, carry us. Though the circumstances have changed over the past two and a half years, the prayer has not.

We were hit by a 17-year old immigrant from Afghanistan. He had topped the rise, and was in the right hand lane quickly overtaking us. The police report said he was doing 80 mph. He was going to collide with the car in front of him (also doing 40 mph, as we had been) but he did not have enough room to slow down and avoid a crash. He opted instead to try to cut in front of us in the left hand lane and zoom around the car he was trying to avoid. He didn't make it. He collided at an angle with the passenger side of our car. His sports car ricocheted off our SUV and continued straight down the road, skidding a long distance due to having lost his left front wheel and the speed he was traveling. As I said above, our car went spinning across the other lanes like a billiard ball. I will never forget the sensation of watching the world spin around me. Nor will I ever forget the terrific jolt that went through us as our car hit the curb straight on at the speed we had been traveling. The impact took out both front wheels. A second later we hit the stone, decorative retaining wall that extended for many yards down the sidewalk. The sudden stop when we hit the wall was the most violent experience of my life. While knowing immediately that we had been injured, my first thoughts were that we had somehow managed to survive that initial crash. It was the first of many miracles we would experience over the next two years. Jan remembers my saying over and over, "What did I do?" Bewildered, for a brief moment I was convinced that somehow I had caused this crash. I had never seen the car coming that hit us and it made no sense to me.

The driver of that car was not hurt, nor was his passenger. The car was a 2009 Nissan 300Z that someone had purchased for him a month earlier. As we were heading to the hospital, I saw him standing beside his car with his hands in his pockets talking to his buddy and laughing. I'll jump ahead and tell you his car was not totaled like ours, and within three weeks he had it repaired and operational again.

The driver was uninsured. His insurance company had cancelled his insurance just a few days before the crash because he was a high risk for them. He had also been ticketed for speeding and reckless driving—all three misdemeanors, which shocked me under the circumstances. He was not taken to jail or even detained. He had lied. It took the police officer a while to determine he was uninsured, and he said he had lost control of his car due to a problem with his left front wheel (a story he concocted while looking over the damage and trying to formulate an alibi). The witnesses would have none of it and stayed long enough to give the police officer the straight story.

We have no idea what this kid was doing at 12:30 PM on that road driving that fast. We learned he was not a student. He was living with several other guys, all older than he, in a rented house about two miles from our home. He had his car towed to that address and parked it in his driveway.

This driver had a history of serious traffic violations, the most recent of which was the previous November. He was pulled over doing 102 mph on the Interstate. He resisted arrest and was charged with a Class E felony. He was not detained for that offense, either. Had he been, he would not have been driving the day he hit us. After the crash, the police officer at our scene was not permitted to check him out on his on-board computer because all three offenses in our case were misdemeanors. He was not allowed to do that due to the fact a violent crime had not been committed. Had the police officer known he was a previously charged felon, he said, later, he would have detained him. As it were, after being ticketed, and arranging to have his car towed, he was free to leave the scene. The police had our destroyed SUV towed to a salvage yard.

Our perpetrator missed three court dates pertaining to our incident and had a warrant out for his arrest, which could not happen unless he was pulled over for another traffic offense. He lost his license for driving without insurance, yet continued to drive with neither insurance nor a license. As I write this, he has been charged with selling drugs to middle school students. I've had many people tell me not to pursue any civil charges against this individual, that sooner or later he will do something which will incarcerate him. His most recent charge is a class B felony that results in prison time between five and fifteen years. As from the beginning, this situation has been in God's hands. I am content to leave it there. Before her strokes, Jan let it be known she completely agreed with that approach. We had too much to endure in front of us to be distracted with all of the facets of retribution.

Chapter 2

THE HOSPITAL

W HEN WE ARRIVED at the hospital emergency room, they
started an IV on Jan. She was held in the hallway for a half
hour then moved to a room awaiting a CT scan. It was obvious she
was seriously injured. The slightest move caused her a lot of pain.
The scan disclosed she had a broken left tibial plateau, a shattered
right ankle, eight broken ribs on her left side, a broken sternum, and
compression fractures at two vertebrae. She also had a head injury
due to the impact. This injury resulted in a case of acute encephalopathy, which, over time, mimicked a severe brain concussion. She
lost short term memory, her cognition was affected (she could not
tell time, nor did she know what day, month and year it was, among
other memory and cognition-related issues). This condition was
referred to frequently in the months ahead following her strokes.
She would go through two months of rehab for this condition. Her
doctors did not know how much she would recover. Her age and
the severity of her injury made it impossible to predict. But one
thing was for certain: if she recovered, her cognition and memory
baseline would be below where it was before the wreck. That turned
out to be the case.

I had no broken bones but had contusions across my chest, an
injured back, bruised wrists and a bruised left knee where, like Jan,

my knee had hit underneath the dashboard. I, too, had a CT scan and was released, though in a lot of pain.

After her CT scan was read, they moved her to the trauma intensive care unit (ICU) where a team of doctors and nurses took charge. Her room was a flurry of activity. By then, Jan was not in much pain due to medication, but was very confused because of her head injury.

She was given a controversial pain medicine called, Dilaudid (Hydromorphone). It's significantly more powerful than morphine. This medication is known for causing delirium. I've had several physicians after the wreck tell me they don't know why this drug is so freely administered. Jan's case was no exception. She was hallucinating for a couple of days, having frightful visions the memories of which remained with her for many months. We did not know what she had been given until we made an issue of her delirium. Late the first night, our son, John, flew in from Denver to be with us. He stayed with her while I went home to change clothes and bring some things back with me that I would need, as I intended not to leave her side as long as she was there. John recognized her symptoms. His wife had been given that drug after some serious surgery and also experienced severe delirium. It was John who asked the staff what medicine she was on. By the time I returned, they had promised not to give her any more of it. Jan also has allergic reactions to opioids, a fact we learned about a few years earlier following her hip replacement, so pain management was a challenge.

We met her orthopedic surgeon. He was on loan to the medical center from a local teaching hospital and was there to develop an orthopedic trauma team. As a result, under his direct oversight and involvement, there were four other surgeons involved in her care in preparation for her surgery. They showed us her scans and we saw the severity of her injuries. The team had to wait three days for the swelling to subside enough for them to operate. During that time they were evaluating the best approach to take.

This turned out to be an issue for Jan. When she had her hip replacement at another major medical center, a university affiliated hospital that is rated as one of the best in the nation, she had the utmost respect for the orthopedic surgeons at that hospital, and managed to tell me she wanted to be transferred there for her surgery. I made the decision to keep her where she was. I had confidence in the surgical team and she was so severely injured that I did not want to risk moving her. She never let me forget that decision. To jump ahead, the surgery was successful as was her follow-up care, but it was a decision that has haunted me to this day. I did not give her what I knew she wanted. It had been a tough decision. In the months ahead, it was a mistake I would not repeat.

Chapter 3

SURGERY AND RECOVERY

B EFORE OPERATING, WE informed her surgical team
that Jan was severely allergic to nickel. When she had her hip
replaced, this fact caused her surgeon there to cancel the operation
until he could prove the hip apparatus they planned to use was free
of nickel in any form. In the meantime, Jan had sent a sample of her
blood to Chicago to be tested (at our own expense...not covered by
insurance). She was so allergic to nickel that the report came back
the next day. Her allergy was "off the chart." This situation caused
the joint replacement team at that hospital to bring all of the medical device sales reps in to tell the surgical team the material make-up
of their particular joints. I remember Jan was called at home by one
of the fellows on that team who thanked her for speaking up. We
don't know the ultimate outcome, but my suspicion is they take
metal allergies even more seriously than I'm confident they had
before. In that case, the medical device they had chosen was in fact,
nickel free.

Her trauma orthopedic surgical team had to order a large
number of metal objects for the surgery, to include the actual plates
necessary, and also all of the various screws. They got most of what
they needed right away, and made sure that before the surgery,

every piece they collected was nickel free. It took them two days to assemble what they needed.

Jan's surgery was scheduled for the third day following her admission. She remained in the trauma ICU. The orthopedic trauma team could not guarantee an operating room scheduled for her would actually be available. Because the hospital is a Level 1 trauma center, if an emergency orthopedic trauma patient arrives and requires immediate surgery, other scheduled patients can be bumped. That did not happen, but her schedule did get accelerated. On the day of her surgery we were told it would occur in the afternoon. That morning, however, she was told that her surgery would happen much sooner. She was wheeled down to the operating suites and prepared for surgery. I was with her. The lead surgeon came in to brief her on what was about to happen and to reassure her they knew what to do and that the surgery would turn out fine. He also said he was glad she had not been moved to the other hospital. We were left alone for about ten minutes. I held her hand and said a prayer over her for her protection and the guidance of her surgeons. Then she was moved into the operating suite where there were five surgeons prepared to operate on her. Her surgery would ultimately take over six hours, which is one reason why all of the orthopedic trauma team was there. They had to share in some of the work due to the anticipated duration.

I went to the waiting room, which was very well organized. There was a large digital screen on which was the status of every patient in surgery. Each patient had an assigned number and that is how they were tracked. Movement was color coded. You could tell at any time the stage of the surgery (e.g., prep, opening, surgery, closing, recovery, etc.).

I had plenty of time to reflect and, again, the situation was overwhelming. I prayed fervently for this surgery to be successful and that Jan would come through it well and, because of its success, she would be perfectly positioned to take the next steps, which were a huge unknown at that point. I was still plagued by the knowledge she had wanted the surgery to take place in another hospital. Without knowing who would have done the surgery, she still believed they would do a better job. So my prayers were especially focused on a very successful outcome, one that would put her mind at ease.

After a couple of hours, our son, John, joined me for a wait that we had no idea would take so long. It was good to have him with me. He had still not come to grips with the situation. Neither of us ever anticipated a time in our lives where we would be seated in a surgical waiting room anticipating what was happening and how long it would take.

After six hours we could tell from the digital screen the surgery was over and she was in recovery. Approximately an hour later, her surgeon came to the waiting room to give us the good news she had not experienced any complications and the surgery portion of her ordeal was over. He kindly showed us x-rays of her knee and ankle before the surgery and afterward. The after images included all of the hardware that had been implanted. It was a formidable sight to see, and it was clear such procedures are very complicated and thus take a long time. They had started with her ankle. With that portion completed, three hours later they started on the tibial plateau (knee). I still have those x-rays.

I was actually joyful. I thanked God for his mercy. So far everything had worked out well.

When Jan returned to the ICU she was clearly not fully recovered; moreover, she was hallucinating...or was it delirium? I didn't ask what medicine she had been given throughout her surgery. Six hours of general anesthesia leaves its mark. She was pulling at the three IV lines that were in her. One had to be reinserted. Eventually a doctor gave her Haldol, which calmed her down. They had also put padded mittens on each hand that looked like boxing gloves, the purpose of these was to prevent her from pulling out her IV lines. She tried to remove them but couldn't. So she resorted to her teeth, actually pulling at one of the mittens, and managed to get it off her hand. For a while, they strapped her hands to the bed rail.

After she was recovered the next phase of her hospitalization began. She definitely needed observation. There was often a nurse in her room for a couple of days. At about 6:30 AM each morning, the orthopedic surgeons would converge in her room to check on her status. Jan had her knee in a brace of sorts that fastened with Velcro. There were two lines coming out or her knee incisions to allow the wounds to drain. That was what they were most interested in, as blood clots were a real risk.

Jan remained in the ICU for two more days. Almost immediately she had Atrial Fibrillation (AFib). Alarms went off and she was put on an IV injection that returned her heart to normal functioning. This happened one more time before she left the ICU. She was on blood thinners to prevent a blood clot, but they didn't stop her from having a pulmonary embolism. That, too, had to be treated directly. These AFib instances, and the treatment for them, would have a big impact a year later when she had her first stroke. I will explain this in more detail in Part III. To make matters even worse, she developed a "C. diff" infection, which resulted in multiple episodes of uncontrollable diarrhea. She was put on a strong antibiotic, but the C. diff continued. C. diff is very contagious. I had to put on a hospital gown and mask to remain in the room with her.

After those two days she was moved to the Transitional Care Unit (TCU), informally known as a "step down unit." She was still on monitors and IVs. The main difference was the nurse to patient ratio was more liberal. Her nurse had four patients versus two. Still, she got excellent care in the TCU. The C. diff did not improve, though, so the nurses had their work cut out for them. For me the TCU was a godsend. That unit was new, the rooms were twice the size as the ICU, there was a comfortable couch I could sleep on, there was an in-room bathroom and shower, and it was quieter, with fewer interruptions. We got to know the nurses in the TCU very well.

In the TCU she had AFib one more time.

After three days in the TCU they moved her to the surgical floor where she remained for three days. I was unnerved there due to the sparse staffing level and the lack of monitors. I didn't sleep much because I felt I had to stay awake for Jan. Often I had to go looking for a nurse when she was in need of something.

When the three days on the floor ended it was time to transfer her to the in-patient rehabilitation hospital. Late one afternoon on a very cold day an ambulance came to take her the five or so miles to the rehab unit. I followed the ambulance in my car. It felt very odd to be leaving the hospital after nine days and nights of my being there. My plan in the rehab hospital was also to remain with her 24/7, but we didn't know what to expect. Things were slow when we arrived, definitely a different pace than the hospital had been. It was a bit eerie, actually.

"Tis very certain, the desire for life prolongs it."
Lord Byron

Chapter 4

INPATIENT REHAB

I T WAS VERY quiet when we were brought into the rehab hospital. A nurse who would soon be off duty, took us to Jan's room. It was a small room but not too far away from the nurse's station. At this time I felt my first bout of depression set in. I felt like we had been abandoned. The room had a sofa on which I would be sleeping for the next 17 days. By then, both my back and my chest were in great pain. My chest was black and blue and had multiple contusions that hurt...a lot. Getting down onto the couch was painful; getting up was even more so.

Jan's C. diff continued for a while longer before a powerful antibiotic knocked it out.

The food in the hospital had actually been good. Jan had a varied menu for each meal and she did not have a single meal that was disappointing. She ate very little of her food, though, and I ended up eating some of it. This was not the case in the rehab hospital. If she was to have food brought to her room, I would be the one getting it. I got her meals cafeteria style. After a few days Jan would have lunch and dinner in the cafeteria, from her wheelchair. What I remember most was that so much of the food was fried, and yet she was on a heart healthy diet. I subsisted for two weeks mostly on bacon, toast, milk, Honey Nut Cheerios and coffee for breakfast, and little else through the course of the day. Jan did not like much of anything there. As the days progressed, I would go to Panera Bread to get her a turkey sandwich and some soup. She ate that. The upside of this experience was that each of us over the month of February lost twenty much needed pounds. The high point of the cafeteria was typically sharing a table with other patients, so Jan slowly began to regain her social skills.

In order to be able to go to the in-patient rehab hospital, patients had to be able to endure three hours of therapy per day. She had been deemed capable of this. The schedule fluctuated and was never predictable, which was difficult for us.

Physical therapy was limited. All they could really do was teach us both how to move Jan from a bed to a wheelchair or to a bedside commode, using a sliding board. That was a difficult skill to master, especially with Jan's leg in the immobilizing brace she continued to wear, and as much overall bodily pain she was in. The physical therapist was a real task master. The two occupational therapists were more congenial. In any rehab hospital their main objective is to help the patient do as many activities of daily living (ADL) as possible. For Jan this almost exclusively focused on cleaning, toileting, grooming and eating. All of these two therapeutic approaches had one aim in mind: Get you out of the rehab hospital and either to the patient's home, or to a skilled nursing facility, before Medicare stopped covering the inpatient rehab expense.

In the hospital, Jan had been (poorly) fitted for a back brace that was best suited for a medieval torture chamber. With two compression fractures of her vertebrae, the neurosurgeon on the trauma team had prescribed a brace that was ridiculous. This was the low point of her entire inpatient episode. I must say, in the nine days Jan was in the hospital, and the seventeen days she was in rehab, she never saw her neurosurgeon, yet his input for her care was the most traumatic experience she had following the surgery. In 2016, Jan had a cancerous tumor removed from her left breast, followed by a seven week course of daily radiation. The breast surgery and subsequent treatment left that area of her body very tender and sore to the touch. Add to that the severe chest trauma that occurred with the seat belt catching her in our wreck, and you can begin to see how a back brace was an agonizing proposition. She would scream and cry every time it had to be worn. If she were to be inclined more than thirty degrees, the brace had to be on. That meant it had to be worn for all therapy and anytime she was in her wheelchair.

I made a big issue out of that brace. The physical therapist was unsympathetic. Her rehab physician was more attentive about the matter. He arranged for a manufacturer's representative (the person who had originally fitted her for the brace in the hospital) to come to the rehab unit and have another go at sizing it properly for her. I never understood why this hadn't been done correctly the first time. The result was somewhat of a relief for her, but she never really tolerated it. She was not followed by the neurosurgeon who had prescribed it. Jan never once complained about any back pain, so she could not see why she needed to wear the brace in the first place. After a while, we would put it on her and not fasten it properly. When worn properly, her breast was so painful that it made therapy impossible. So we made a show of it rather than follow the letter of the law.

There was another element of therapy at the rehab hospital—speech therapy. In Jan's case, she did not have any speech or language processing issues. What she did have were major cognition and short-term memory issues. She could not read an analog clock. A calendar meant nothing to her. It was difficult for her to read or write. She could not add up change given to her. She couldn't count or do simple arithmetic, among other tasks. There were numerous cognition exercises she had to perform, as well as some short term memory tests and exercises. I instinctively knew by then that her broken bones would eventually heal and she would be able to regain most of her mobility after months of outpatient rehab. But her mind was another issue altogether.

The acute encephalopathy she suffered really manifested while in the rehab hospital. We did not know just how seriously her brain was injured until they began to assess her. None of her doctors or therapists would make any predictions as to how much improvement we could expect, or how long it would take. What they did predict (accurately) was that even with a lot of therapy, she would not return to her pre-wreck "baseline." I took her in her wheelchair to speech therapy but would sit outside the office where she was being treated, out of sight, so as to be able to listen in and discern for myself just how severe this problem was going to be. Jan was very self-conscious about my being there. Her mind is "private property" to her. She has two master's degrees and a PhD. I like to tell her friends that she got her PhD and her Medicare card in the same month (age 65). She is the quintessential life-long learner. In the twenty years she spent as a teacher, most of it was teaching academically gifted students. As a child, she was a gifted student. In 1968, she was the first girl in the history of her high school to be chosen to be president of her honor society. I have to say I had many a conversation with God about this situation. If Jan had lost her cognition entirely, she would never emotionally recover. With every speech therapy session I prayed hard she be able to beat this. She didn't want me to know how serious this problem was (though I did). She was embarrassed.

We would see these same symptoms reappear after her first stroke. Even the therapy she received from the speech and occupational therapists turned out to be some of the same exercises she had to perform while doing in-patient rehab after the wreck. All of the neurologists who have treated her have been very upfront as to how the encephalopathy compounded the problems with her strokes. I have estimated to others that following her wreck-related speech therapy, she perhaps made it to 85 percent of her pre-wreck baseline. For a person with her mind, that was a major issue.

While in the rehab hospital, Jan was injected with Heparin twice a day. This is a powerful blood thinner. Upon her discharge, I opted to not give her injections but for her to take her blood thinners by mouth instead. She was prescribed Xeralto, another powerful blood thinner which she would be taking for the next three months.

We remained in the rehab hospital for 17 days. We made it clear that upon discharge, we wanted to go home rather than to a skilled nursing facility. That was a fortuitous move. An ambulance van came to get her, wheelchair and all, and take us home. I had spent a day away from her getting the house ready for her return. I turned our den into our room, rented a hospital bed and wheelchair and had to purchase a bedside commode and bedside table. I bought new sheets and a nice bedspread in an effort to make her new living quarters as homey as possible. We gathered our things, said our goodbyes, and left with great relief. We felt we were ready for the next phase, whatever that was to entail.

Chapter 5

HOME

———— ⟨∞⟩ ————

T HE DAY WE arrived at home was a bit overwhelming. We
had talked about how much we wanted to leave the inpatient
rehab facility and wanted some peace and quiet with no interruptions. We also chose to say goodbye to the back brace. Her back did
not hurt and she felt the risk was worth it not to have to continue to
endure the agony it caused. That turned out to be the right decision.
She never had any noticeable problems with her back.

Despite my attempt at organizing the den and making it attrac-
tive and homey, there was much about hospital beds I didn't know.
The mattress was extremely uncomfortable. I didn't know at the time
that when you rent a hospital bed, you can also rent an air mattress
that circulates air and can be adjusted for the desired level of firm-
ness or softness. After just a few days, Jan's back and bottom were
hurting her. I'm sure that her back injury was partially to blame, in
retrospect, but the mattress was the real culprit. I chose to attempt
to tackle the comfort issue with lots of folded up blankets on top
of the mattress and under the fitted sheet. This helped some. The
bed had to be manually raised and lowered, though the tilt of the
bed could be electrically controlled with a device attached to the
bed. No one told me when I was renting the bed to address the comfort issue head on. We were fortunate that she did not develop any

bedsores while she was at home. Also, Medicare would not cover the rental fee for an electronically raised and lowered bed (The reason why would baffle me; it makes no sense, and I, her caregiver, had a back injury.) so I had to painfully hand crank it each time (several times daily). Later, when she had her third stroke and came home, I paid the $118 per month it took (out of pocket) to have an all-electric bed.

Our friend, Ken, a pharmacist, knew of a foam rubber cushion that looked like an upside down egg carton, and he bought us one. That improved the comfort level of the bed, but there was a downside that made it impossible to use. To leave the bed for the bedside commode or her wheelchair, and to be moved back again, we had to use a sliding board. This was under the best of circumstances difficult to use, but it would not work with the cushion. For the board to work, the bed had to be firm to allow the board to be level with the chair. It had to be held down forcefully by me in order for her to use it. Holding the board down and helping her move was impossible with the cushion. With her leg injury, it was extremely painful at times for her to use the board. Her ribs were still sore, too. In order to use the board effectively, I had to remove the cushion. The bed remained uncomfortable as long as she had to use it. An air mattress would likely have created the same problem.

Using the commode was something she never got used to doing. She could never reconcile the fact I had no problem cleaning up after her. She found the whole thing degrading and depressing. For me, the only problem with the commode is that when she had to use it, often the need was urgent. Getting her from the bed to the commode, or from the wheelchair to the commode, was often a race against time.

We spent the time mostly reading and talking. The topic was a recurring one: Where do we go from here? Both of us were still perplexed we had not been killed in the wreck. God was with us for sure. There were several ways the crash could have ended our lives. Our car hit the curb head on instead of sideways, which would have flipped us. We narrowly missed a telephone pole. Had we hit that, especially sideways, we would have died. Two cars missed us as we spun across their lanes. Had one (or both) of them hit us that would have been fatal. We could have been hit and then driven either sideways or head on into the wall. We kept playing the "what if's" in our minds. Our conclusion was the same as we had discussed in the hospital and in rehab. God was not finished with us on this earth. So the next part of the puzzle was to try and figure out what he had in store for us. We eventually stopped talking about it. The immediate challenges facing us were too daunting to look that far into the future.

One of her favorite things to do was to have me read daily inspirations from the book, *Jesus Calling*, by Sarah Young. At first, I followed the calendar of daily readings, then I chose to look through the book to find readings that I felt better fit the kind of day she was having. She really liked for me to read from that book. Doing so brought a visible expression of peace over her. She would often ask me to keep on reading, or read something again that I had recently read. We also used the Episcopal *Book of Common Prayer* and read from the Daily Office. At night we would often say "Compline" together to end the day. I prayed over her every day and anointed her with holy oil often. These were special times for us as we had never done any of these things before.

During Christmas I had hung a plaque on the mantle of our fire place. It simply said, "Believe." I had left it there on purpose after Christmas but didn't know why. Now that we were home it took on a prophetic purpose. Whenever she showed the slightest sign of discouragement, I would point to the plaque and ask her to tell me what it said. That usually had the desired effect. I know every time

I saw it I had to let it speak to my heart as well. Faith in the future propelled us. We were curious to know what God had in store for us.

Going to church was not a viable option. We arranged to have someone from our parish come by weekly to visit and share the Eucharist with us. This was always something we looked forward to. By this time the word had gotten out regarding our predicament and we learned that many people were praying for us. Our biggest support system was the Racine Dominican sisters in Wisconsin, and also the many associates belonging to that Order. Jan and I had been Racine Dominican Associates for fifteen years. There is a sizeable group of associates in St Louis, to which we belong. Sister Carla Mae Streeter, OP, was one of Jan's professors when she was getting her master's degree in theology at Aquinas Institute of Theology. Carla Mae had gathered a nice size group of committed associates. This was the only such group of its kind. Most associates live in and around Racine, Wisconsin. We were constantly in their prayers and we had visitors to our house from the group.

We had been attracted to the Racine Dominicans because of their mission, "Committed to truth and compelled to justice." So it was easy for Carla Mae to "recruit" us. At the time we joined this group, both Jan and I were very committed to several social justice causes, one of which was ending the war in Iraq. They were silently amazed that I, a retired Army colonel, had become an anti (Iraq) war activist. I had even flown at my own expense to Washington, DC, to protest the war with hundreds of other Christians who assembled in a snow storm at the National Cathedral and then walked down Constitution Avenue to the White House to finish the event. This made me a very minor celebrity with the group.

Sister Carla Mae has been with us throughout Jan's hip replacement, her breast cancer, the wreck ordeal, as well as all of her strokes. She has become my spiritual director. We talk frequently. I rely constantly on her wise counsel. There are many sisters in Racine who are also committed to us. We are blessed to have their prayers and support.

Our main goal was to have Jan recover sufficiently for us to be able to leave the house and do outpatient rehab physical therapy. That required home health care. We had arranged for this level of support before leaving the inpatient rehab facility. It would consist of physical, occupational and speech therapy. They typically came to our house twice a week. The downside was that there was no set schedule. They would call us the night before and basically tell us when they would arrive. This took a lot of coordination. Often I had one therapist coming in as another was leaving. Medicare and Tricare paid for the service, but it does not go along indefinitely. The patient is assessed and then therapy is supposed to move you to a higher level of functionality. For physical therapy, until Jan was able to stand (she was non-weight bearing for three months) there was little more the therapist could help her with aside from some leg strengthening exercises we learned, and ensuring we knew how to use the sliding board under every homebound situation. The physical therapist discharged her early but would return once again when Jan was weight bearing.

Occupational therapy was to ensure Jan could do as many activities of daily living (ADL) as possible in her situation. This did not take long to determine. Aside from her inability to walk, she was rather self-sufficient. The therapist did not remain with us long once that was determined, and Jan was discharged from occupational therapy.

We had a person come by twice a week to bathe her and wash her hair. I had been giving her a bed bath and had been washing her hair in the kitchen sink from her wheelchair prior to our getting the help. We continued to use the kitchen for hair washing while her baths continued to be bed baths.

Early on in our home bound state, speech therapy was the most needed and sought after therapy. Speech pathologists are trained to do a lot of things with regard to communication and cognition. In Jan's case, cognition and short term memory were still issues due to her encephalopathy. She had worked very hard on this while in the inpatient rehab facility, but more therapy was needed. Fortunately for her, each time the therapist worked with us at home, Jan continued to improve. It was a very happy time for me to see her regaining that brilliant mind of hers. She also fed on her own success, wanting to do even better the next time. While she would never reach the baseline that existed before the wreck, she would be able to show marked improvement. The way the therapy works is once the patient "plateau's" the therapy ends. This happened about six weeks into our home health care. I remember her speech therapist telling me Jan had "graduated." That did not mean, however, she had recovered to her pre-wreck cognitive baseline, but she was much better and able to function somewhat normally. Once the therapy had ended, Jan was encouraged to continue to work on her own, which we did.

On April 26, 2018, three months from the day of the wreck, we took Jan to Saint Louis University Medical Center to meet with her orthopedic surgeon who had returned there after working with the orthopedic trauma team that operated on her. This was a big day. I have it recorded on my phone. I brought Jan's walker from her hip surgery with us. We placed it in front of her wheelchair and the doctor told her to stand up. She did so without a problem. I have to say this was one of the happiest days of our lives. We could begin to see the light at the end of the tunnel. She took a few steps around the office and did not need to sit down for any reason. She was pain free, as well. The doctor said he wanted to see her again in a month and we should go home and practice, advising her not to do too much too fast.

It was during that fateful office visit that I asked her surgeon about Jan's need to continue to take the blood thinner, Xaralto. He wanted to keep her on it a while longer. I wanted her off of it, for reasons that were not clear to me at the time. God spoke to me and told me she needed to be off of it, so I insisted. We agreed we could take her off Xaralto and put her on a daily regimen of 81mg aspirin, instead. In retrospect, I wish we had not given her the aspirin, but I had no reason to object at the time. It was better to me than her remaining on Xaralto. That day she began taking the aspirin daily and did so until March of the next year. He had told me the reason he wanted to keep her on the drug was due to her having had a pulmonary embolism while in the hospital. I did not recall that at all. When I later reviewed her 63-page discharge record it turned out that his memory was sound on that score. She had an embolism—a small one—that no one in the hospital had told either of us about. That irritated me to no end.

Until that day, whenever we had to leave the house for a doctor appointment (which was several times during those two months), we had to call for a transportation service that would put her in the van while still in her wheelchair. She would be strapped in and I rode in the back with her. This was always an anxiety producing exercise. Jan was unable to get out of the chair and into a restroom should the need arise, so we had to time her appointments and transportation around her likely bathroom schedule. A few times this turned out to be agonizing for her. The van would be called to pick us up and take us home, but we never knew how long that would take. It was a big deal for both of us when leaving the doctor's office after she had stood for the first time she had to use the bathroom. I found a handicapped bathroom, wheeled her into it, put her walker in front of her and she got up and did what she needed to do. I helped her back into the wheelchair for the ride home, but she was under no stress for the long ride that day. We fully appreciated at that point what a blessing mobility really was.

Now that she was able to walk with a walker, the next thing for us to do was to get her to outpatient rehab therapy. In order to do that, however, she would have to be able to go up and down two steps into and out of our garage so she could get into our car. Our 2016 Honda CRV had been totaled in the wreck. I bought a 2018 CRV without even driving it. The first one had kept us alive and I figured why not get another one! I was so busy helping Jan at home I was unable to go to the dealer to pick it up. Finally, the sales rep was kind enough to drive the car to our house, two months after I bought it, and give me the new car operational briefing in our driveway. He was very sympathetic to our plight. This new car would turn out to be just the right height for Jan to enter and exit it for trips out of the house.

It was at this time our home healthcare physical therapist came back to the house to work with Jan to be able to negotiate those two steps. That turned out to be easier for her than we had anticipated.

On May 17th, I received a call from our son, Michael, wishing Jan a happy 68th birthday. During the call he asked what I was making her for dinner (knowing we could not yet go out). I was actually prepared for that question and said I had bought a couple of steaks and was going to cook them on the grill on our deck. He said he would surely like to do that with us and said I would need to get another steak for him (laughing). I said that would not be a problem were he here. Next thing we knew there was a loud banging on our glass door to the deck. The blinds were closed and I couldn't see outside. I was startled, and Michael asked over the phone, "What was that noise?" I told him I was getting up to go check the door and see who was banging on it. The banging continued...louder. When I opened the blinds, there stood Michael with his phone in hand, laughing. What a wonderful surprise that was! He had flown in from San Antonio to surprise his mother. When I let him into the house he looked around the den and could see we had everything under control and it was actually sort of nice in there. That, he admitted, took a load off his mind. He hadn't a clue what to expect but probably suspected the worst. Earlier, he and John were worried I could not possibly care for Jan and wanted me to put her in a skilled nursing facility (to which I had flatly refused). Once he saw how we were making it so well, he was very pleased. By then Jan was using her walker well. He took little time in telling John we were doing fine. I went to the supermarket and bought another steak. We had a great two days with him. I was very moved he made that trip and surprised us. He improved my morale greatly and Jan was delighted to see him.

Chapter 6

OUTPATIENT REHAB

I T WAS A big day when Jan was able to climb two stairs of our staircase, turn around and go down the same two steps. She did that repeatedly. The therapist, who was a great motivator (especially when working with someone who is inherently motivated—like Jan) said, "OK, Jan. Let's move to the den and go down the two steps to your garage." Recently, I had installed two handles on the doorjamb to the door. That way, she could hold on to the handles, going out and coming back in. She went to the door, opened it, and easily let herself down to the garage. We then went to my car and I opened the passenger door and encouraged her to get in. Using the overhead handle on the passenger side, she pulled herself into the car and exited just as easily. This had all taken about three weeks of therapy to get to this point. We were now ready to roll!

I had previously gone to the Mercy outpatient rehab facility near our home, and did the preliminary paperwork necessary for when Jan would be ready to start. The physical therapist assigned to her was a very personable, competent, and funny fellow. He's a terrific motivator and was very encouraging.

The day of her first appointment Jan used her walker to get into the facility. Her therapist assessed her and worked with her a couple of times with the walker. She then moved from the walker to a cane. After a few meetings, he would take her cane away when she arrived and have her walk and do other therapy without it, just using a gait belt he held onto as needed. Jan's orthopedic surgeon had encouraged her to use a cane for the rest of her life, even if she did not believe she needed it. His logic was sound. The one thing he did not want to see happen after all we had been through was for Jan to fall (or get knocked down) and break her hip. He also said that people would naturally defer to her if they saw her with a cane, and be less inclined to unintentionally bump into her. So she carried a cane and it turned out to be true. People saw her cane and would defer to her so she could get around relatively risk free.

Jan was head majorette of her high school marching band and was also ranked number two in the State of Tennessee for her baton twirling and dance routines. At 68, she still knew how to twirl a baton (especially one that was not on fire at both ends). She began walking in to see her therapist with her cane in her hand, twirling it and passing it in motion from her right hand to her left and back again. He thought that was funny. It was another thing that gave her confidence.

The therapy routine was for her to practice doing the types of things that would be required of her out in the world. She climbed and descended stairs. She walked up and down a sloped ramp. She stepped up and down mock curbs of various heights. She stepped over objects of various sizes. She walked around a small indoor track as many times as she could in a certain span of time. She went outside, weather permitting, and walked around the parking lot and in the grass lawn. The timed walk around the indoor track would become one of the test skills she had to demonstrate every four weeks so that the therapist could measure her progress. There were several other skills she had to master, all against the clock. As long as she continued to improve her times, therapy could be extended.

This went on from May through the end of December. By then she had reached a plateau where she was typically hitting the same times on all of her tests. I had filmed her climbing stairs and racing around that track. I still have them in my phone. It is both inspiring for me to look at them, and sad at the same time. She will never again be able to do that. She was actually in better condition than she was before the accident. She had dropped 25 pounds and her balance and her gait were also better than before.

Jan had a lot of fun working with her therapist. He was a confirmed bachelor, younger than our youngest son, and she was always asking him if he had a girlfriend yet. One day, near the end of her therapy sessions, he said he did. He had been rooming with another guy and decided to move out and get his own place. (He said the guy's dog didn't like him. I think the feelings were mutual.) This all happened near the end of her therapy. We never learned how that all worked out.

It was right after she began rehab that we began frequenting the local Catholic Charismatic Renewal parish again. Known as The Shepherd's Table, this group of about a hundred people meets every Saturday night in another church's building. Every second and fourth Saturday they have an active healing ministry following the mass. A cadre of about a dozen parishioners spend an hour or so after the service working in pairs to pray for the healing of the sick and injured. We had begun attending these meetings two years before, about the time Jan had been diagnosed with breast cancer. The Saturday before facing her surgery (a lumpectomy of her left breast) we asked for prayer and healing of this stage two breast cancer. That next week when she had her surgery, the doctor came to the waiting room to tell me that the surgery went exceedingly well. The tumor was standing alone in her breast, but she said it was only a couple of millimeters from the chest wall. She was able to carefully remove it entirely. She also removed one of Jan's lymph nodes to see if the cancer were present in the lymph system. When the test came back, the lymph node sample was free of cancer. The next step was for her to undertake radiation therapy six days a week for seven weeks. After all of this was done, she was declared cancer free. We attribute these results to the healing prayer she received just a few short days before her surgery. We came back to them on a couple of other occasions for healing and deliverance prayers for ourselves and to also pray for others with them.

Early in Jan's outpatient rehab we had asked for their prayers again, this time to help her recover completely. Jan was a remarkable success story in therapy, exceeding many peoples' expectations. God was with her in this recovery, giving her the confidence she needed to benefit from her therapist's excellent care. It could have gone either way.

While Jan had been an in-patient in hospital rehab, she said to me that once this ordeal was behind us, she was making a vow to herself to spend the rest of her life only engaged in things that brought her joy. I thought that made a lot of sense, and if anyone deserved it, she did. She went on to say that she was happiest when years before we had been members of the Church of Saint Michael and Saint George. I said that, I, too, had fond memories of our time as members of that congregation, and that I also thought it would be good for us to re-join that church. We made the move in late summer of 2018 while she was in outpatient rehab. Jan was able to join the ladies of the church a couple of months later when they hosted one of two annual ladies spiritual retreats. She was very happy at the conclusion of the retreat and we were in agreement our spiritual life was getting back on track.

At the end of December, Jan was reluctant to give up her physical therapy. She even asked if she could come back less frequently. Of course, she had "graduated" and that would not be necessary.

January of 2019 was the beginning of our new start. She was thoroughly healed and ready to get on with her life. It had been a long ordeal, but not without its benefits. We had grown much closer as a couple through this experience. Our two sons had seen us making it just fine in our den, and even saw her in therapy. The future looked bright. This lasted less than two months...

Part II

—— ✥ ——

FIRST STROKE

Chapter 7

FIRST STROKE

———⟨◦⟩———

L OOKING BACK ON it, the signs were there that something ominous was happening. While Jan was doing so well in her physical therapy, some of the cognitive issues associated with her encephalopathy had not gone away and seemed to be reappearing. Our sons asked me privately if she was getting dementia. I refused to admit it, and made excuses for her, all the while having this nagging feeling that she was having some cognitive difficulty. Two signs involved her laptop and her iPhone. Each summer, she would order new school book bags for each of our grandchildren in Texas. The bags were of their favorite colors and each was embroidered with their name. She had placed orders on-line for these bags several years in a row. It took her just a few minutes. In 2018 she was having difficulty doing this on-line, saying that her computer was not functioning properly. I volunteered to make the purchases for her and had no difficulty. She had done her PhD dissertation on that laptop; she knew how to use it. Other situations involved her iPhone. She was unable to do something which she had done without an issue many times in the past. She said her phone was acting up. I would take her phone and do whatever needed to be done and comment that I had not experienced whatever technical difficulty she was experiencing. I thought these situations odd, because she had mastered both devices, but did not probe or make an issue of it.

Thanksgiving came and went. She was overwhelmed by having to get our house ready for company. She could not find certain recipes and would get exasperated. I would go to the likely places and after wading through a lot of unusual disorganization, find what she was looking for, but that took hours that we simply didn't have to spend. Christmas came and went, too, with similar issues that were new experiences for us.

January 2019 was a difficult month. She began to take out her jewelry and kept counting the items to see if they were all there, something she had never done before. She would be unable to find something and get agitated. I would get agitated, too, because losing these items was a real risk. I could find them, though. In February this situation got worse. She actually did misplace some items that I had a very difficult time finding, but usually did, and in odd places. She also began wanting me to purchase reading glasses for her. She accumulated twelve pairs of them, and would get argumentative with me if I challenged her on the need for those purchases, and she would count them to ensure they were all in her possession. She often got exasperated because she was sure she had lost some of them. It was no need for me to ask her why she felt she needed so many pairs of glasses. She took to putting them all in a soup tureen in our dining room, then miscounting them. I repeatedly counted them for her and they were always there. She bought several tote bags from Vera Bradley and began to put all manner of things in them with no rhyme or reason. She would insist on carrying all of them in the car with her wherever we went; not knowing what was in each bag. I would sneak looks into the bags and they were mostly filled with much of nothing. She would get very irate when I suggested she take only one bag or just a purse and make sure what she needed was in there. Or take one bag and put her purse in it, anything to keep from carting five bags around which were an easy target to tempt someone to break into our car. There were other examples of similar behaviors, all of which came on over a short period of time.

I began to suspect that these behaviors were attributable to her head injury and that some complications were emerging. I refused to tell myself she had not recovered to her pre-wreck cognitive baseline. I was too focused (we both were) on her significant progress with physical therapy.

Physical therapy had officially ended in early January, less than a year from our wreck. The last week of February she became very confused. She again took an obsessive interest in knowing where all of her jewelry was. I again was concerned she would lose important pieces. I had not yet put the items into a safe and she was able to get them and sort them at the dining room table. Without going into more detail, suffice it to say, I became very concerned about her behavior that week. She was highly irate and argumentative, none of which was normal for her. Clearly her mind was being affected by something. I thought it was only related to the wreck, refusing to believe it was more than that. She refused to sleep, obsessing about several things. One night she woke me at 3:30 AM elated that she had found her wedding ring. I didn't know she had lost it. She had been down in our dining room, again, counting her jewelry. When I told her that she needed to get a grip on things, she began accusing me of controlling her. That was new.

On February 27th she became psychotic (or so it seemed to me) and left the house still in her pajama top and sweat pants, clutching her coat and all five of her tote bags, and went to a neighbor's house saying that she wanted to get away from me, all the time stressing that I was controlling her. That was the point at which it became clear to me that she was having some sort of serious mental breakdown and needed help—fast. The neighbor took her (at my request) to a psychiatric hospital run by a psychiatrist whom I trusted. She wouldn't go with me. I wanted that doctor to evaluate her. When she arrived she went into the "intake" office and two individuals determined that she was having psychosis. I had arrived at the hospital while she was still being evaluated. By then she had calmed down and began acting as if nothing had happened. The psychiatrist recommended she be admitted. Jan came out of the intake room and calmly but firmly told me she wanted to go home. I reluctantly agreed to take her home, but aside from her calm demeanor at that point, she was clearly still in distress.

That night it all started again, confusion surrounding her jewelry and the perception that I was controlling her. Late the next morning she left the house again, not properly dressed, without a coat, with five tote bags in hand yelling that she had to get away. Two of our neighbors knew by then she was having some sort of mental distress and calmly convinced her to go back to the psychiatric hospital, taking her there themselves, and staying until well after I arrived. She was in worse shape than the day before and that time I reluctantly had her admitted. Unfortunately, the psychiatrist, whom I was relying on, had left town for a meeting the day before, when he had wanted to admit her, and would be gone for three more days. Had I admitted her the day before, he would have had time to evaluate her, then, rather than five days later. If I had known he was leaving town I would have. I regretted that. She ended up suffering needlessly.

Jan was unmanageable on the psychiatric floor. She was psychotic by the looks of things and was incessantly talking and wandering. When I went to the floor to check on her she begged me to take her out of there saying, "I don't belong here!" Ultimately, no truer words had ever been spoken, but at the time I believed I had no other option. She had been diagnosed with psychosis and was being medicated for that, to no effect. She spent the next three days hardly sleeping at all, and continued non-stop talking and wandering the floor, agitated. The staff had asked me not to visit her on the floor because she became even more unmanageable when I was there, begging to leave. I spoke with the psychiatrist in California nightly by phone and he assured me that the house physician was observing and treating her, and communicating with him and that upon his return, he would check on her immediately. At that point he didn't expect seeing anything more than psychosis due to the reports he was being given.

When he returned from California, he checked on her first thing the next morning. I was coming into the hospital when she was being carried out by an ambulance crew. The doctor had determined after only a few minutes with her that what she was experiencing was not psychosis, and she needed a neurological work-up, quickly. The ambulance took her to the nearest hospital. Our son, John, had arrived the day before and we went to the hospital together. In the emergency room she was immediately referred for a brain CT scan. When the scan was evaluated, the ER physician informed John and me that Jan had had a stroke. I was stunned, yet overwhelmed by the knowledge at that point that she had not been having a mental breakdown at all. I felt guilty that I had not done something different, sooner. I regret that to this day. I asked the physician what caused it. He said her scan showed she had experienced a hemorrhagic stroke in her right temporal lobe. He showed the scan to me so I could see it. When pressed by me for a cause, he said he and the radiologist suspected a condition known as Cerebral Amyloid Angiopathy (CAA). He said it was a toxic protein in the vessels of her brain that could cause spontaneous leaks (hemorrhagic strokes). The fact that she was 68 at the time, and the stroke was hemorrhagic, led them to that hypothesis. I was told that only seventeen percent of stroke patients have hemorrhagic strokes. The vast majority are Ischemic strokes, caused by a blood clot in the brain and not a hemorrhage. The nature of her stroke was that she began to hemorrhage a few days before (they could not determine for sure how far back) and as the hemorrhage progressed, her behavior became more acute. By the time of the scan, she had stopped bleeding, but they could not tell me when that had started or stopped. The scan did not show a new or evolving bleed.

I began to punish myself for not having handled this situation differently. I must admit, a stroke was not something I had even remotely considered. While I had not committed the common signs of a stroke to memory, some of the telltale signs one hears about include sudden dizziness or loss of balance, numbness or weakness of the face or limbs, and trouble seeing clearly (see the Epilogue for more information). As it turned out, she HAD demonstrated signs of a stroke—just signs I was unaware of—mainly, an "altered mental status" such as confusion and agitation, sudden behavioral change as well as disorientation and not making much sense. I took only a modicum of comfort in knowing the psychiatric hospital staff had not identified a stroke, either. That really surprised me though. She had begun to have it about the time she was appearing to get psychotic at home, and it appeared she had begun to have the stroke at least five days before it was diagnosed. The intake people at that psychiatric hospital should have at least suspected a possible stroke and evaluated her for that.

She was taken to the intensive care unit at the hospital.

Chapter 8

HOSPITAL, INPATIENT
REHAB, AND HOME

A S HAD HAPPENED with our car crash, I mentally prepared myself for a long and uncertain ordeal. I was also not going to leave her side, so prepared to stay in the hospital as long as she would be there.

I was told, repeatedly (even later in the in-patient rehab hospital) that we should count our selves fortunate. Jan could walk and talk. Talking is what she did a lot of, though, due to stroke-related anxiety and agitation. The staff gave her a variety of medications designed to calm her down and even get her to sleep. They were largely ineffective. They later started her on Buspirone for her anxiety and it seemed to work.

One thing that was soon apparent to me was I was not going to be getting any substantive information out of the ICU and house physicians (I had not seen a neurologist.). This became a trend in the months ahead with her subsequent strokes. Neurologists typically had no definitive answers beyond her diagnosis, while I, on the other hand, had lots of questions. I could comprehend the challenges of broken bones and trauma, but a brain injury due to a stroke was not something I could readily understand. Without help from people who should have been available to speak with me, I went to the Internet to get as many answers as I could. That is a practice I have pursued before and continue to this day. I was able to do this, and still do, but it makes me sad to realize that so many spouses or other caregivers faced with similar problems are not accustomed to doing in-depth Internet research and wading through all of the technical language to get answers that are typically unavailable to them by healthcare professionals (for one reason or another).

I learned that a stroke in the right temporal lobe would affect primarily four things: Short term memory, cognition, emotions, and behavior. The cognition deficit I could understand given the events of the past week; memory, too. The behavioral and emotional issues were also understandable, to include extreme agitation. It would not be until a week later when the full impact of her short term memory deficit would become apparent.

I also looked up Cerebral Amyloid Angiopathy (CAA). Her condition at that point was suspected but not verified. This was the beginning of a great deal of research I would have to do over the next several months, especially after her second and third strokes. CAA is an incurable and untreatable condition. While not rare to physicians, especially, neurologists, neurosurgeons, and radiologists, there are a lot of details about CAA that remain largely unknown except to isolated research centers that are studying the condition in depth. No one had suggested CAA ran in families. None of her relatives had ever suffered a similar brain disorder. Her father had a mini-stroke (ischemic) but had recovered. The truly bad news, aside from the condition being untreatable or incurable, was if this diagnosis were proven to be correct, she would be at high risk for having another stroke (or more).

I was deeply troubled by all of this. Aside from the obvious seriousness of her condition, after all we had experienced the previous year, and all of the prayer we had done and had benefitted from, and the conclusions about the future we had assumed, this was a major blow to my faith. We had asked ourselves while Jan had been in hospital rehab following our wreck, why we had survived that horrific crash. Our conclusion was simply that God was not finished with us, that there were more things we had yet to do. We assumed that those things would involve us both, and that we would have several more years to do what God intended for us to do. Jan has a PhD in theology, a master's degree in theology, a master's degree in education, and has been trained and certified (and is very experienced) in spiritual direction. Years before, I had attended a four year "theology by extension" program offered by the School of Theology (Episcopal) at the University of South (Sewanee). The program is called Education for Ministry (EfM). I graduated after four years and became a mentor in the program for four additional years, leading my own groups. Between her formal preparation and mine, we believed our future direction would be directly tied to our theological education and training and in some yet to be determined, ministry.

The realization that our plan for the future had for all intents and purposes been dashed against the rocks was a spiritual crisis for me. The unfairness of it all, and the waste of her preparation, talents, and gifts, was hard for me to accept. I had long bouts of prayer over this and pleaded with God to help me make sense of it all. That wasn't fast in coming.

At that point I had not yet come to grips with the severity of her stroke and how that would most likely affect her ability to function in a vibrant ministry. Over the next three months that would be made clearer to me. The pathos of it all was more than I could bear at times.

So while she was in the hospital, we focused on each day and what we would be doing next. Neither of us had any idea what to expect. In-patient and outpatient rehab for a stroke were fuzzy prospects to me at that point. I had seen stroke patients rehabilitating at the outpatient rehab center when Jan was recovering from the wreck, but most were having mobility issues, which she then did not have.

As soon as she was stabilized, we began discussing next steps. That would be in-patient rehab. The question was, where? She could have gone anywhere. By the time of her first stroke, Jan had changed most of her physicians over to the Barnes Jewish Christian (BJC) Healthcare System. After what we had gone through with the wreck, I was going to make the earth move to keep her this time in the BJC system. I knew that would be what she wanted. Progress West Hospital was a satellite hospital of the BJC system. Discharge planners began asking me where she would want to go. BJC had two rehab centers. One was in downtown St Louis near their major medical center, and the other was in another BJC satellite hospital in St. Peters, Missouri. The downtown facility was very large; the St Peters facility had about thirty patients. Moreover, I was told the St. Peters facility had all private rooms and had a neurologist on staff. I wanted both so chose St. Peters. After about a week in the hospital, she transferred to the St. Peters in-patient rehab facility. Due to her having a private room, I was able to arrange to stay with her 24/7, and had a couch to sleep on.

By and large, the St. Peters facility was a good place for her. The neurologist there was not at all encouraging, though, and had no real interest in answering my perfectly appropriate questions. He never mentioned Cerebral Amyloid Angiopathy. When I brought it up he dismissed it as though it were not important. He was focused on her rehab and getting her out of there as soon as possible. That said, the internist who was the rehab physician, had a work station right across from Jan's room. He and I struck up a good relationship and he was extremely helpful, going out of his way to keep me informed. He also collaborated with me with regard to her anxiety, agitation, and sleep medications. Jan would be up virtually all night and the nurses would put her in a wheelchair and take her with them down the hallway as they went about their duties, room to room. I tried to sleep but was unable to do so knowing she was out of the room, being disruptive and getting no rest. The doctor and I finally agreed on a sleeping pill (Rozerem) and continued the dose of Buspirone for anxiety. Eventually, she would sleep for a few hours each night. The biggest problem with her not sleeping was that she would be exhausted each day and was unable to make the most of her therapy, the most important of which (as it was after the wreck) was speech therapy for her cognition and short term memory issues.

Her speech therapist was excellent and she was very collaborative with me. She could only work with Jan for an hour a day, five days a week. Due to Jan's erratic sleep schedule, we made most of her appointments for the afternoon. The therapist had numerous cognition and memory tools and exercises for Jan to do. We had lots of downtime on our hands and I asked her if she would provide me with some of those exercises and tools so I could work with Jan on them in her room when she was not otherwise in therapy. She readily agreed to this and provided me some excellent material. I was able to put these to use, daily. Jan made some progress with her therapy, but it all depended on whether she was alert enough, and rested enough to fully participate, which was difficult with her sleeping problem.

There were many stroke patients in that rehab facility (which was another reason I chose that hospital). I recall how I thanked God that she appeared to not be as incapacitated as so many of the other stroke patients.

One day we had to share her speech therapist with another stroke patient due to a scheduling error. That gentleman was confined to a wheelchair and had aphasia. That was my first experience with an aphasia patient. Aphasia manifests in different ways depending on where in the brain the stroke occurred. It involves a left hemisphere injury, usually in the left temporal lobe. Aphasia blocks speech and language processing. What often comes out when an aphasia patient speaks is gibberish. They refer to it as "word salad." This fellow's speech was 100 percent gibberish. What troubled me most is that he knew this and wanted so much to be understood. I could tell he was very frustrated. Some aphasia patients, in addition to expressive aphasia, have receptive aphasia as well, meaning that language coming in to them is indecipherable. This patient did not have that added complication. His aphasia was limited to speaking. I remember the words the rehab physician had said to me several times: I should be grateful. Jan's symptoms were not so severe, and she could walk and talk. He was right. After spending some time that day with the aphasia patient I did thank God that Jan was spared that condition. We have a very rich history of meaningful and loving conversations.

Occasionally, I would need to leave the rehab hospital for a few hours, mainly to prepare for her return home. She would get very stressed when I was not there. The staff had gotten accustomed to my being there to attend to her during therapy down time. I elected to contract with a home care agency to provide a sitter to be with her when I was gone. Jan was not happy with this arrangement. I remember her telling me it was very frustrating for her as she had little in common and nothing to talk about with the two sitters with whom we worked. But separation anxiety was clearly a part of it. When I was out of the hospital she couldn't wait for me to return and would have the sitter call me a few times to ask where I was and how much longer I would be gone.

We were getting near the maximum amount of time Medicare would cover for her stay at the in-patient rehab facility, so it was time to get serious about the return home. Not knowing how much help I would or would not need, I contracted with the same home care agency to provide people to stay with us at our house in case I could not care for her adequately myself. By then, Jan was starting to object to taking her anxiety or sleeping medicine. She was convinced she was fine and didn't need it. This was not the case. The rehab physician wrote out prescriptions for medicine she needed, but we would be unable to leave with any. It would require my stopping at Walgreens on the way home to have them filled.

The day we were to leave I was in for a big surprise. We could not get Jan into our car. She became disruptive and unmanageable, creating a disturbance. I had very little help getting her out of the hospital and into the car. Fortunately, she began to calm down enough for me to be able to drive the twenty miles home. When I told her I needed to stop at the drug store she loudly objected. She became so agitated that she tried to exit our moving car. It was all I could do to steer the car and keep her in it at the same time. Fortunately I was near Walgreens and pulled into the back of the parking lot to get her to calm down. She didn't. In the end I had to call 911 to come and help me, dialing the phone with my left hand while holding on to her with my right. The paramedics arrived and talked her down and asked me what she took for this condition. I told them I needed to go into the drug store to get it. She was already overdue her medication. They helped me by keeping her company while a police officer and I went into the store to fill her prescriptions. The paramedics got her to take her anxiety pill immediately. Everyone waited around a while. By the time she had calmed down we were ready to go the rest of the way home. I was very afraid of what to expect next, and prayed hard that this situation not get further out of control. It was well after lunch by then and she said she was hungry so we decided to get lunch. She was behaving fine until we were near finishing our meal and she had another panic attack and was very unruly just outside the restaurant. I could not persuade her to get into our car and she was, again, very agitated and disruptive. Again I called 911. Again we went through that day's ritual of calming her down. Then we arrived home.

When she entered the house she panicked again, this time because she was convinced we were not in our own house and she was frightened. This time I was able to calm her down, but it was hours later before she began to believe she was in her own home. Before she came home I had removed all of her valuables and put them in a safe deposit box. That night we had a home care attendant who would remain with us overnight and be relieved the next morning. That first night Jan slept with me in our bed for the first time since her stroke. It was a challenge for me to get her to take her sleeping medication but she finally did...and slept all night. After three days of having a care attendant, I cancelled the service. Jan was getting accustomed to being at home, was sleeping, and was much more manageable.

She was convinced that she had left our house to go to someone else's house in the neighborhood who had stolen our cat, Sasha. This was a story she often told. She was convinced this had happened, though she never mentioned who these people were. Sasha had never been out of the house and had been cared for by a neighbor while Jan was in the hospital and rehab facility. This story got more elaborate with each telling. She really believed that had happened.

Over the next two months we had some good days and bad days. In the first month home Jan became enraged about nothing and took her rage out on me. On two occasions I was hit hard and my glasses were knocked off each time. ALL of this behavior was totally out of character for her. In 49 years of marriage I had never seen anything like it. There was nothing to be done but let these episodes pass, which they usually did after a few minutes. It was almost like a seizure. On two occasions, however, they were so severe that I had to call 911 again. On one of those occasions she had bolted out of the sliding door to our deck and headed for the rail and was beginning to climb over, saying that she was going to jump (nine feet to the ground) when I was able to stop her. That time the paramedics took her to the hospital. As the ambulance was leaving she was beginning to calm down. She only spent one night in the hospital for observation, but while there they did an MRI of her brain. It was then that she was confirmed as having Cerebral Amyloid Angiopathy. In addition to the lesion in her right temporal lobe, she showed over thirty "micro-hemorrhages" spread throughout her brain. These appeared as very small black dots on the MRI. These micro-hemorrhages were confirming of her diagnosis. We knew for certain at that point that she was at a very high risk of having another stroke. Most CAA patients eventually do.

After that hospitalization and we had returned home, I had a long conversation with her saying that these bouts of rage had to stop. Strangely, at that point, she calmly agreed. Without any prompting from me, she apologized profusely and promised never to do any of those behaviors again. I had no way of knowing how long that would last, but as it turned out it did last. She never did anything like that again. That day sitting out on our deck, she looked at me and with all sincerity said, "You know, I could not have made it this far without you." I said something I wish I could take back. I said, "Yes, Honey, you're right. You couldn't have made it this far without me." I was pretty exasperated by that point and that was a terrible missed opportunity to say and do the right thing. If I had it to do over, I would have gotten out of my chair and walked over and hugged her and with all my heart said that it was all OK, I loved her more than life itself, and I would do anything for her. She is my life. But I missed that opportunity. It makes me very sad as I write these words to have to recall that day.

Despite that missed opportunity, it was the beginning of some good times. She did calm down, how I do not know. God? I certainly prayed hard that she would. She never again had any type of rage or outbursts. It was time to move forward with the next steps... again, back to the outpatient rehab facility.

Chapter 9

OUTPATIENT REHAB

W
E WENT BACK to the same outpatient facility where she
had done all of her physical therapy following the wreck.
She required all three therapies this time: speech, occupational, and
physical. Her physical therapist took up the PT mission again. She
did not need to regain much use of her body. He began working
with her twice per week and then said if we wanted to, she could
reduce it to once per week. His aim was simply to keep her from
losing the progress she had made before her stroke. She chose to
continue with two, mainly because PT was really the only therapy
she wanted to do. She said early on that speech and occupational
therapy were a waste of time. She called it, "too simple" and "child-
like." It wasn't at all. I had been down that path before not a year
earlier with the wreck, but then she knew that she really needed it.
This time she was not convinced, though it was especially true.

From a cognitive and memory standpoint, her stroke symptoms
were almost identical to the encephalopathy from her head injury.
Her short term memory, though, was really off. Her basic cognition was as well. With the wreck, Jan had been unable to tell time
using an analog clock, or know what day, month and year it was.
She could also not count change. It was the same with her stroke.
Both the speech therapist and occupational therapist doubled up

on her, making the most out of her time by giving her very similar exercises to do. At first, she did not want me even in the room. As before, her mind is her identity and she did not want me to see her having to struggle. In the end she thought differently and actually wanted me in there with her. So did her therapists.

As with the hospital speech therapist, I asked them to give me exercises I could do with her at home. Jan actually preferred this to going to rehab. She called it, "homework," often asking me to do it with her. And often that was late at night when I was very tired and she wasn't (she has always been a "night owl"). I worked very hard and patiently with her to get her to be able to tell time again and know the day, month, and year. We did numerous other memory and cognition exercises. I even bought my own exercise binders through Amazon. She was the model patient with me. She knew I was really on her side and trying my best to help her. I actually look back on those times with a bit of fondness. She was very apprecia-tive and we worked well together. It was even somewhat fun. We did these exercises on our love seat in the living room. She would cozy up next to me and really try to do her best.

Jan had always wanted to learn how to play the piano. Her speech therapist at the rehab hospital thought learning to play the piano would be excellent therapy for her. I completely agreed. We brought that up to the outpatient therapists and they both agreed and strongly encouraged her to get and learn to play the piano. Jan launched into this project with enthusiasm. We looked around for a used, spinet piano and found one that was on consignment at a large music store specializing in pianos. One advantage to buying it there was they really wanted first time piano purchasers, especially adults, to learn to play quickly. As a result, they offered unlimited piano lessons for free at their store in eight-week sessions. That was a deal too good to pass up. We bought the piano and had it delivered and put it in our living room against the front wall. It was a nice looking instrument in good shape. She cleaned and polished it and would sit on the bench touching the keys, thinking ahead to the big day when her lessons would begin. The lessons would not start for three more weeks. She was looking forward to it and instinctively believed all the complicated brain activity associated with reading music (which she did already) and having to translate the notes through her brain and into her hands and onto the keys, would be the best possible therapy she could do for herself. It made perfect sense to me. I knew she would give it her very best effort. Aside from the therapeutic value, it was always something she had wanted to do.

As a child she played the clarinet in her high school band. As a teacher for twenty years she mostly taught academically gifted middle school students. One day they were challenging each other to learn to do something they had always wanted to do. They each had to make a commitment to do whatever they chose. Her students asked her what she had always wanted to learn. Jan said, "The flute." They held her to it. She rented a flute and took to it so well that she upgraded and bought a much nicer one. While taking lessons she had to do a recital in front of about a hundred people. I was with her that evening and have never been more proud of her. It was yet another proof of the kind of person she has always been—determined to succeed at anything she puts her mind to. I was convinced she would give the piano the same treatment. My only concern was whether her stroke would make that more difficult than she thought.

We would never get the chance to know.

While she was recuperating from her first stroke, we had been regularly attending the Church of St Michael and St George (Episcopal). The ladies at that church have two spiritual retreats each year. She had attended the one held the previous fall while recuperating from our wreck. She was looking forward to the one in June. Preparation for that retreat created a new problem for her at home. Jan takes a lot of medicine for various conditions she has had over the years. For the previous year I had taken on the responsibility of setting her meds aside and giving them to her morning and night. She was not cognitively capable of keeping them straight on her on. In addition, I was also giving her the stroke-related medicine for anxiety, memory, and sleep. Jan had two choices for the retreat: she could attend at the retreat center and stay overnight, or she could commute. I could take her and pick her up that way. Commuting would make it easy for me to continue to give her the medication and she would be safer. She wanted to remain overnight and yet she was panicking about keeping her medicine straight. Against my better judgment, I put her medications into several separate envelopes that were clearly marked with the contents and when she was to take them. She also had the complication of her short term memory deficit. The three days leading up to the retreat were very stressful for us. I was very concerned about her going to that retreat and staying there.

In the end, it didn't matter.

Part III

———— ✌ ————

SECOND STROKE

Chapter 10

SECOND STROKE

—————⟋⟍⟍⟋⟍—————

T HE EVENTS LEADING up to June 6th, 2019, were more of
the same. We were still struggling with the decision of how
best to accommodate Jan's wishes regarding the ladies' retreat which
was scheduled for the next day. That morning, she was disoriented,
but not unusually so (at first). Jan was still upstairs in her night
shirt while I was in the kitchen, drinking coffee. I heard her call
my name in mild distress so I went up the stairs and saw her wandering around our bedroom. She was saying, "I can't find my context. Help me find my context." I asked her what her context was,
and just guessed she was referring to her contact lenses which were
downstairs on the kitchen table, not in our bedroom. Putting them
on each day was an ordeal and had to be done sitting at the kitchen
table with a mirror, and a chandelier over the table, all supervised
by me. Applying her make-up was also done there, and was equally
as challenging.

She came down the stairs and sat in front of me at the kitchen
table. She said, four or five times in a row, "So, now what are we
going to do?" When I spoke to her that was all she would say. At
that point my heart sank, for there was no doubt after what I had
learned with the first stroke, that she was having another one. My
worst fears were being realized that these hemorrhagic strokes in her

case evolved. They were not sudden crises like when a clot hits in an ischemic stroke. She was deteriorating, so I went over to her and hugged her closely. I quietly told her that she was having another stroke and I was going to have to call an ambulance. I called 911 and took her upstairs to help her put some clothes on. That was unsuccessful, because she was very agitated about dressing. When the ambulance crew arrived, she was not dressed and the paramedics had to wrap a blanket around her as they put her into the ambulance. Off they went to the hospital. I threw some things together as quickly as I could and jumped into my car to chase the ambulance. I arrived at the hospital about fifteen minutes after she did.

When I went into the ER the staff knew I was coming and had a pass prepared for me and directed me to Room 13. When I arrived at the room, there were four people with Jan trying to get her calm and into a hospital gown, as she was still not dressed. She was very frantic and scared. The urgency of the look on her face when she saw me will forever be etched in my mind because of the sheer helplessness of her situation. She called my name, desperate for me to join her by the gurney. She broke free of the nurses' grasp of her hands. She grabbed both of my hands and looked at me with the most urgent look on her face. She said, almost shouting, "I love you so much! I love you SO much!" It was as though she instinctively knew that those might be the last words she would say to me. I told her how much I loved her and tried to help the nurses get her calm so they could take her for a CT scan.

I followed her to the CT room and helped them get her on the table. She was so restless they had to give her two injections of Haldol, a strong sedative. After the scan, it was about a half hour later when the radiologist and the neurologist on the stroke team came to me and said she had another stroke. This one was to her left temporal lobe and was larger than her first stroke to the opposite side. The neurologist said they were trying to figure out why she had this stroke only three months after her first one. The interval between strokes was very unusual.

I didn't know it at the time, but those "I love yous" were going to be the last purposeful words she would say to me for a long time. This stroke had taken out her speech and language processing center. She now had aphasia. When this happens in your world it is a devastating diagnosis. In 49 years of marriage we had never had a day when we could not freely communicate.

That is when the car wreck raised its ugly head for the first time since before her first stroke. They had looked at her hospital computerized medical record from the wreck and noticed she had been on very strong blood thinners for four months and on aspirin every day after that up to her first stroke diagnosis on March 4th, 2019. Cerebral Amyloid Angiopathy, hemorrhagic strokes and blood thinners are a bad combination. We would hear this again...more than once.

The nursing staff wheeled her to the neuro ICU. It was across from the trauma ICU where we had been a year before. I had to wait for an hour until they had her settled into her room. Then I moved in for the next ten days. She would spend half that time on the neuro floor.

The procedure when a hemorrhagic stroke patient comes to the ICU is to schedule another CT scan a few hours later to confirm that the hemorrhage has either stopped or expanded. She had that CT scan and it confirmed that the lesion had not expanded.

As with all ICU patients, the nurse-to-patient ratio ensures that the patient gets a great deal of attention. She even had a sitter nurse in there with her from time to time. She had IV lines in both arms, as before. Jan has a history of pulling lines out of her arm. The staff tried in vain to stop this. The solution is pitiful to see. As was the case after her surgery a year before, she had cotton padded mittens put on each hand the size of small boxing gloves. There was no way she could grip a line with those mittens on. Also as before, Jan was resourceful; she figured out if she struggled long enough, she could remove one of the mittens with her teeth. Once they saw her doing that, she spent a few days with them strapped to the sides of her hospital bed.

This stroke had created another problem we had not previously experienced—she was incontinent. That created another whole set of problems. Her mental state and her incontinence meant she would have to be changed on a regular schedule. She had pads underneath her to make the changing process faster and easier, but I knew this was going to change how she was cared for in the future and would be far more involved than moving her to a bedside commode via a sliding board. I would also need help. That was a sobering thought.

I was waiting for her to develop AFib again. We would have had to face the blood thinner question once more. Fortunately, she did not develop that or C. diff during this hospital stay. She did, however, develop a nasty bed sore. This required a wound specialist to come in to treat her, and the staff had the added challenge of applying a protective ointment and a bandage over the wound.

After several days she was transferred to the neuro floor. The staff on that floor was very accommodating to me. They placed her in a room next to the nurses' station and it had enough space in it for them to put an extra hospital bed in there for me to sleep on. I had sadly become accustomed to being by her side 24/7 in these crises.

This second stroke took me down. While I was constantly seeking clinical information, and weighing the dismal projections (or lack of a projection whatsoever) I had plenty of time to be alone with my thoughts. This was especially true at night. There was my sleeping wife and me in a dark room. I was awake with God. I talked with him a lot. Rather than simply resigning myself to a terrible fate, I went through a series of changes, from despair, to faith, to hope, and then to sheer determination. That phase was only possible through my faith in God. He has never forsaken me or Jan. While I could not see clearly into the future, or even know if we had a future, I exercised faith and hope. In this case, hope was not wishful thinking it was a confident expectation which fueled my determination. God was doing his part. She had suffered a second stroke and yet she was still with us. He was with me every step of the way. He gave me the assurance I needed that every step I took, and would take, on Jan's behalf, was the right step.

I rank ordered sources of credibility. God was first. The Holy Spirit speaking through me and empowering me was second. And medical professionals were third. I cinched up my belt another notch and got down to the business of being faithful in everything I needed to do. I asked God to show me what to say or do or even think, and then embolden me to go about it without wavering. I listened for the Holy Spirit to tell me whom to listen to and whom to not, whom to seek out and whom to ignore. I made the faithful decision to take everything a person in a white coat told me with skepticism. They had to say what they said. That was not only part of their training, but it was the culture of hospitals. See the patient, acknowledge the spouse, check the patient, make computer entries, make a pronouncement, answer questions only superficially, and move on. There were few exceptions to this routine. The Holy Spirit, on the other hand, was always there guiding me, patient and full of insight. The choice of whom to listen to was not difficult. It has remained that way to this day. I knew God was holding on to Jan. The specter of Cerebral Amyloid Angiopathy was always there, and doctors say, truthfully, that we just don't know what will happen next. Of course we don't! Their training says to tell me to expect the worst. The Holy Spirit tells me, "Hold it! Not so fast!"

Beginning the previous year when she was in the inpatient rehab hospital, it became readily apparent to me that patients need strong advocates. I found the nurses worked with me whenever I had a concern. Those concerns usually involved medication dispensing. If a physician orders a medication, even if it is to try something for a day or so, the medication typically remains on the dispensing list until an issue is raised with the physician who prescribed it and it is removed by the doctor from the list. I had to do this on a regular basis at the rehab hospital, but not so much in the hospital. Nevertheless, it is something that was necessary everywhere she went. Jan takes a lot of medications and has been doing so well before the wreck and her strokes. Getting that medication placed on her orders took some coordination. I had to be on top of the situation to ensure she continued to get her standard medications in addition to the new ones, and also ensure medications were not dispensed if I knew they should no longer be.

During this stay in the hospital I went to the hospital chapel several times a day to pray. I was so distraught I actually prostrated myself before the alter begging God to help her and help me make some sense of all this tragedy. I did not get answers, but did find a modicum of peace. I had to remain strong and I prayed hard for me to be the rock she needed and not let her down in any way.

Stabilization and eventual discharge from the hospital were the goals. The staff began working with me early on regarding Jan's status. I wanted her to go to the medical center's inpatient rehab hospital this time because I had learned that there were several stroke patients there and the staff had a lot of experience working with them. In order to be able to go to inpatient rehab the patient has to be able to endure three hours of therapy per day. Jan was too weak for most of the time we were at the hospital to be considered for the inpatient rehab facility. She was evaluated daily. All of the therapists and the hospitalists were involved in that decision, along with a nurse practitioner who represented the rehab unit.

Jan's sleep issues arose again. She would be up talking most of the night and would be in an exhausted state by morning. For a long time I was unaware that insomnia is a very common affliction for stroke patients. At least a third of them either can't sleep, awake after just a little sleep, or both. No doctor has ever told me this. After agonizing for hours over the past year dealing with sleep issues, it was the Internet where I learned what I should have been told from the start. While it would not have helped her condition for me to know, it would have helped me to at least know why we were facing a sleep problem.

When she was on the neuro floor she had two hospitalists who rotated through her room. They tended to come by to see her between 7:00 and 8:00 AM. When they were there the regimen was to see if she could respond to commands. She couldn't for two reasons: one was the seriousness of her condition, and the other was the nature of her aphasia. She was not processing information effectively. Her diagnosis was Global Aphasia, again, something I had to confirm on the Internet, which is also known as "fluent" aphasia. She was able to speak some words or phrases in English, but most other sounds were gibberish. That is the expressive form of aphasia. She also had a receptive form. It was questionable how much she understood of whatever was being told to her or asked of her, thus her inability to respond to commands.

Over a few days we were fortunate in that Jan appeared to be able to understand some of what was being said to her, sometimes, but she was not responding to commands, which was essential if she were to go to inpatient rehab. If therapists could not get her to respond to commands, there would not be much they could do for her. She surprised me with the occasional English phrases she could say. They were somewhat purposeful early on. One day she said something unexpected while smiling at me, "I love you. You're so cute." I was wearing a blue shirt that she liked. I'm told it is impossible to determine from a stroke how much or how little communication will be affected. I am grateful to the hospitalists who were working with her. They made every effort to prepare her for inpatient rehab. They knew her going there was very important to both of us.

Chapter 11

SKILLED NURSING REHAB

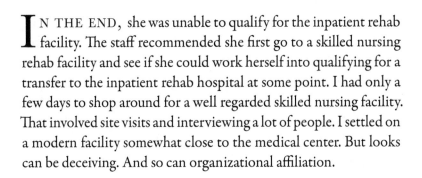

IN THE END, she was unable to qualify for the inpatient rehab facility. The staff recommended she first go to a skilled nursing rehab facility and see if she could work herself into qualifying for a transfer to the inpatient rehab hospital at some point. I had only a few days to shop around for a well regarded skilled nursing facility. That involved site visits and interviewing a lot of people. I settled on a modern facility somewhat close to the medical center. But looks can be deceiving. And so can organizational affiliation.

Once she arrived by ambulance at the skilled nursing facility I had selected, I was in for a big letdown. Over the past year and a half I had grown quite accustomed to having lots of registered nurses around Jan all the time, and physicians coming and going, as well. This was definitely not the case where we went. Even though I had been told it had a very good reputation, as skilled nursing facilities go, it was still unnerving. The staffing consisted of a Licensed Practical Nurse (LPN) over each wing, assisted by a couple of certified nurse's assistants (CNA) to care for numerous patients in constant need of a lot of attention. There was one medical technician with the responsibility to dispense medications to all of the patients on the floor. This turned out to be a nightmare. I had to constantly intercede to ensure they had the right medications for her and she was getting only what she was supposed to get and in a timely manner. The CNA's, with two exceptions, were often hard to find, and if you needed them, you had to go looking for them. Jan was incontinent, and she needed help frequently. She was also still fighting the bed sore she picked up in the hospital.

The therapy she received was minimal. Her care was most often performed by therapy assistants. The allotted time was supposed to be 45 minutes per therapist, per session. That wasn't much. Rarely did a session go that long, and often the PT and OT assistants would work on Jan together, thus depriving her of a dedicated session with one or the other. The exception was the speech therapist. She was the only one on staff and she gave it her very best when working with Jan. The problem was Jan's speech condition, not the effort and skill of the therapist. She did the best she could, but we did not make much progress. I remember being elated when the therapist wrote with a marker on a white board she carried the words, "How are you?" Jan looked at the board and said, "How are you?" The only other things she said when reading was, "I love you." or, "I like you." She has read very little of anything since then, and cannot write but only a few letters, with maximum assistance. This is typical for patients with Global Aphasia. If they could read and write it would be much more possible to communicate with them.

The staff wanted all of the residents to eat in the dining room. Most were wheelchair bound. I spent many hours per day pushing Jan around the facility in her wheelchair. Aside from therapy and meals, there was little else to do. When it was not too hot, we would sit outside in the garden. The main point of doing this was to keep her out of her room. When it was time for a meal I would wheel her into the dining room. Most of the patients there were also in wheelchairs and it was very crowded. Getting to a table and away from the table took a lot of jostling around of wheelchairs. We usually sat across from a couple of ladies who were sisters. One was a

Parkinson's disease patient and the other was her caregiver who, like me, was there for the duration, and slept in her sister's room. She would take it upon herself to wheel her sister to the dining room or to therapy, but they spent most of their time in their room. Her caregiver was devoted to her sister's well-being and was frustrated every day over some legitimate complaint. We got to know them well, and they were very nice, friendly, supportive, and encouraging of Jan.

At that time, it was difficult for Jan to feed herself, so I would feed her like I did in the hospital. She was required to have a soft diet for the entire time we were there. The head server in the dining room did the very best he could under the circumstances, but it was difficult to stay ahead of the workload and also to keep his cool. He was perpetually frustrated. The people he had assisting him did not have their heart into the task. I would typically go to the kitchen to get her food and drink due to the disorganization and delays.

At another table were several very old ladies who typically sat together, one of whom seemed to always be watching us. One day she called me over to her table and said, "Son. We've been watching you with your wife. It is wonderful how patient and loving you are with her. It's obvious you love her very much." I thanked her and listened further. She said I reminded her of her grandfather (this lady was 94 years old). I was curious as to why. She said that her grandfather loved her grandmother very much and her grandmother was an invalid toward the end of her life. Her grandfather doted on her every minute of the day and was very loving and caring. She said she and the other ladies thought Jan and I were a good example of how married people should treat each other in every situation, and especially in such a trying time as the one we were in, and we inspired them. The other ladies agreed. That little talk came at a good time for me. I was not feeling particularly effective at caring for Jan due to all of the hassles we experienced during the typical day. In retrospect, however, I recall what a herculean effort I was making to maintain my composure and patience—not at Jan, though. Caring for her was the easy part, but doing so in the midst of all the frustrations I had with the staff was the challenge. I did everything I could to avoid letting her see that I was frustrated.

One morning I had a confrontation with the medical technician who was dispensing medications that day. I refused a medicine (for good reason) that Jan was scheduled to have received that morning. The technician got very irate with me and said I did not have a right to refuse the medicine, only my wife could. I let her know in no uncertain terms that Jan was unable to speak for herself and that her cognition was very impaired even if she could and that I was speaking for her in every situation. That lady refused to give Jan her medicine after that encounter and said I would have to go to the nurse, instead. She was angry because I was preventing her from "doing her job." When she was on duty she never again tried to give Jan her medicine, always sending me on a search for the LPN who, unbeknownst to that individual, was responsible for dispensing it. This meant her medications which were always dispensed late, were dispensed even later. This was one of many issues I had with the staff.

Often, the CNAs were nowhere to be found. Even the LPNs would occasionally complain about how unreliable they were. Which I felt was a legitimate complaint on their part but not something they should be telling me. They should be resolving the problem instead. I was already frustrated enough. Not all of them were a problem. There were two CNAs who were excellent. I marveled that they still worked there because they were clearly overworked due to other CNAs not doing their jobs.

One thing was very clear to me, as it had been earlier in other less extreme situations. It was absolutely necessary that I be there with Jan all the time. I shudder to think what her care would have been like had I not been there. One of Jan's neighbors across the hall had a similar situation. Her son had to check on her every day (he was younger than me and still employed with regular hours). He made issues of many things and said he would look out for Jan if I needed to be away. He was very nice and also very frustrated.

The rehab physician assigned to Jan was superb. She made every effort to make herself available to me. I was really grateful to her for that and for her disposition and competence. The other two physicians on staff had very bad reputations.

There was a chaplain on staff who was very good at his role, too. He met with us several times. I was distraught most of the time and would open up to him when he was with us. We had some good, spiritual discussions. I was open about my not being able to understand why God would have us in this situation, especially after surviving the wreck the previous year and an earlier stroke. We were convinced as I have stated previously that God was not finished with us, which was, we believed, why we were spared. I was focused on the "doing" of God's work—work we were unable to do and most likely would always be unable to do. He said much of what the elderly ladies at lunch had said to me, that perhaps God had intended to use us as an example to anyone around us as to how a godly marriage should be. Witnessing, he said, takes on various forms. Ours was simply not a form we anticipated. He had his own issues about how the world was coming apart and that none of the things that should be sacred were readily observable in this day and age—especially marriages. He made it clear that we were serving God, just not in the way we had always intended. I did not want to hear that—but he was right. (I wouldn't be writing this book, otherwise.) He made a powerful case. He prayed with us. I remember asking him not to tell God that his will should be done. I made no apologies for asking him to pray that Jan be healed and, especially, have no more strokes. Mine was the only will I wanted honored. I couldn't bear the thought of losing her, and we had clearly lost a great deal, already. Strokes are so cruel.

I've been surprised to learn that people who do not have a loved one afflicted by a stroke (or more) rarely know what having one physically and mentally entails. I mentioned earlier that when we were in hospital rehab after her first stroke I had encountered aphasia for the first time. When Jan was in outpatient rehab after our wreck, I saw the struggles several stroke patients were having and told myself that, were Jan not in rehab for our wreck, I would have minimal understanding of the ravages of strokes and how severe and permanent the symptoms can be.

The fifteen days we spent in this facility were the low point of every experience we have had throughout this stroke journey. There was a nursing home wing there. On her wheelchair rides I would take her to the nursing home section. The care we got in the skilled nursing section varied very little from the nursing home area. The main difference was in the amount of therapy Jan got where we were. I've already said how underwhelmed I was with the therapy. One thing became crystal clear to me: By the Grace of God, I was going to do everything within my power to keep Jan out of a nursing home and take her home with me. I made good on that promise as I will discuss in the chapters ahead. That decision has made all the difference for us. I'm fortunate I am not working and had the means to do this.

I was in constant communication with the nurse practitioner overseeing transfers to the inpatient rehab facility. The lead occupational therapist supported my goal and was working with me to attain it. The overall therapy manager said in a note to the nurse practitioner at the hospital rehab facility that, in his opinion, Jan should already be there. My head, as had usually been the case in my life, was in the future. In an Internet search I had discovered a place in Florida where they have an intensive rehab program—a resident program—where they specialize in aphasia. My long range goal was to rehabilitate Jan sufficiently to be able to take her to Florida. Incontinence was the only hurdle I could see (a BIG hurdle). That is indicative of where my head was. I saw every setback as temporary, and had to always have a solution in front of me—a long range plan. A few months later I learned that I must live life one day at a time. This was a hard lesson for me, but a good one, long overdue.

One idea I had was to hire a private speech therapist to work with Jan once we got home. I had not experienced any speech therapists in an institutional setting that had the time to really work with her. Aphasia is a stubborn problem. Most people never recover from it, others only recover marginally. With that in mind, I went searching the Internet for private speech therapists in St. Louis. I was not making much progress when one therapist, who returned my phone call, said she only worked with children, but knew of someone whom, she believed, would be exactly the person I had in mind. I called that person. Her name is Ruth. She is an aphasia specialist. She said that she did do private duty speech therapy part time. I asked her if she would come to the skilled nursing facility and meet with Jan and me. We arranged a meeting for 7:00 PM one evening. I met her with Jan in her wheelchair, in a conference room near the entrance. Our meeting went for two hours. Jan was in rare form that night. At the time, she was again having the problem of talking incessantly when she was anxious or agitated, symptoms of her strokes. When she was in that state, she could not be quieted and was talking in an animated way with an imaginary person. Getting her medicine to stop this was, as I have previously stated, difficult at best. Ruth tried in several ways to get through to her. She told me that in her view Jan was hallucinating or something like that. She said she could work with the aphasia, but not until she could engage Jan directly and calmly and establish and maintain focus. We both wondered if this would ever be possible, but we agreed to an hourly fee for service and planned to reconnect once we got home. I was feeling better that I could be proactive where her aphasia was concerned and not have to remain at the mercy of institutional providers. We would meet her again.

Jan's physical therapy was always much shorter than I wanted it to be. It consisted of having her get out of her wheelchair, stand up with her walker, and walk around the room. Occasionally, the therapy assistant would put a "gait belt" on her so she could walk unassisted other than with the belt she was holding. A couple of days the therapist had her walk up and down five stairs four times. While Jan was unable to respond to commands, in her mind she knew what to do when she encountered stairs. I wanted to work with her when she was not scheduled for therapy, as she was clearly not getting enough.

We had an incredible amount of down time, and I was working diligently to get her to the inpatient rehab hospital. Every day in the skilled nursing facility mattered. Frankly, I couldn't wait to get her out of there. I got a lot of push back on working with her myself. The PT assistant didn't trust me. I told her that I had been working in physical therapy with Jan for over a year and could handle it. Finally, I had to get the therapy manager to approve it. I was able to have Jan walk up and down the hallway in our wing with her walker, then with me holding on to her gait belt, and finally, doing it with just one cane. She was able to do this with little difficulty. She got a lot of positive reinforcement from other patients on the floor. I was very pleased with her progress.

One day Jan was lethargic and running a fever. It took us two days to get a urine sample and another two days to determine that she had a urinary tract infection (UTI). This, understandably, affected her therapy. She was put on a course of antibiotics and we tried to continue with her therapy. After a few days, Jan could no longer perform the basics in her routine. Her therapists, and I, thought it may be due to her UTI. I was in contact with the inpatient rehab facility and had to tell them we had suffered a setback. The nurse practitioner agreed to "follow" Jan for a few days. We all were working toward a move to the inpatient rehab facility.

We were in the therapy room one afternoon and Jan could not get out of her wheelchair and up onto a walker. The previous day she had labored to get to the stairs and was unable to take the first step. The day she could not get out of her chair unassisted was a difficult one. Two therapists got her up and into her walker. I could tell her left hand and arm was weak as it was quivering. She was only able to shuffle for a few steps and that was it. We had her wheelchair right behind her and had her sit back down. My instincts told me we were in trouble. I let my incurable optimism convince me she was just weak from the UTI, but she only had one more day to go on her course of antibiotics, and the previous few days she had been able to move adequately.

After therapy was over I wheeled Jan to another wing in search of her doctor. Jan was slumped over asleep in her chair, which was unusual for her. I found the doctor and we discussed the problem. We both hoped it was just weakness from the UTI. The doctor said to me that, "We shouldn't dismiss the possibility that she has had another bleed." This was a Thursday, she suggested that we wait until Monday and see if she were any better. I pushed back and said if there was any chance that she was having another stroke I did not want to wait four days to get her to the hospital. She said if we called an ambulance and took her to the ER they would do a CT scan immediately and we would know for certain. If she had not had another stroke we could bring her back to the skilled nursing facility. I steeled myself for bad news, but still was hopeful that she was just having a setback.

The ambulance came and took her back to the hospital. We waited in the hallway, with Jan on a gurney, for over an hour before she could be seen. She did not appear to be in any distress. Finally they took her out for a CT scan. A half hour later the ER physician came to me and said, "I'm sorry to have to tell you, Mr. Burroughs, but your wife has had another stroke." My heart sank. Despair flooded over me. The doctor said, "We can't understand why she has had three hemorrhagic strokes in four months. We looked at her computerized record and noticed that she had been on a lot of blood thinners going back to her admission here for your auto accident." Given that she had Cerebral Amyloid Angiopathy, they guessed that the culprit could only be blood thinners she was on the year following her surgery and up until her first stroke. I asked her where this stroke had occurred in her brain. In essence, it was in the motor cortex at the top of her head. She said this explained why she was unable to stand or walk for the previous two days. Once again, Jan had been having an evolving hemorrhagic stroke. The doctor said she was very sorry and that they were going to move her to the ICU. As I watched them wheel her away, I followed and could not help but grieving. Our world had come crashing down, again. All of my hopes about getting her recovered and into a residential aphasia program and hopefully functional again in six to twelve months went right out the window. It was easy at that point to get frustrated with God.

Part IV

——— ∙◆∙ ———

THIRD STROKE AND
THE HOSPITAL

Chapter 12

THIRD STROKE AND
THE HOSPITAL

———————— ·⟨๑⟩· ————————

T HE ROUTINE WAS becoming all too familiar to me. Go
into the patient waiting room and sit there until the nursing
staff in the ICU had set her up—gowned, IV lines, etc. When they
came to get me I tried to keep up my spirits in front of Jan. But this
was a very bad sign. And I was running out of feigned optimism.

Again we settled into the routine. I was not surprised when a
few hours later they took her to the CT scan again to see if the
hemorrhage was getting any larger. That report showed it had not
expanded from their initial observation.

My time in the ICU with her is a blur. I had simply spent too
much time in there, and as I look back on it, some of the things I
remember may have been from previous admissions to the ICU. I
ordered her meals for her and fed her each time. For a few days they
had a nurse sitting in with us much of the time to keep an eye on her.
These nurses were temporary staff who were highly skilled and were
a bit surprised that sitting with Jan was all the ICU team wanted
them to do. I was grateful for their being with me.

When he could make himself available the ICU physician was very accommodating. When he came in one afternoon I asked him if he could spend a few minutes with me answering my questions. He graciously agreed. The first thing I wanted was to see her CT image on the computer screen that was in the room. He called up the radiologist's report, read it to me, interpreting some of the language, and then called up the screen. I could see the hemorrhage. It ran along the groove that separates the two hemispheres of her brain, the longitudinal fissure, and extended slightly into the right hemisphere. I remember thinking it odd that this hemorrhage ran a few inches along that groove, rather than extending out into more of a circular image as her other two strokes had done. This explained why her left leg and arm were affected by the stroke.

I would make a point of being there when the ICU staff, fellows and other physicians were making their rounds from room to room. It was always the ICU nurse assigned to Jan who would brief them. It was hard to listen to. They always stressed her age, her underlying disease, other diseases, her previous two hemorrhagic strokes, and her overall condition (vital signs, etc.) and that she was "full code." There was never any cause for optimism. The looks on the faces of those being briefed was always deadpan.

Her first afternoon in the ICU, following her second stroke five weeks previously, the neurosurgeon on the stroke team was looking in on her and wanted to talk to me. During that conversation he had asked me what I knew. I was able to spout off some information about her Cerebral Amyloid Angiopathy and, by then, her likely diagnosis of aphasia. I remember that he had asked me if I were in the healthcare profession. I did not count my years in the Army Medical Service Corps as being a healthcare professional. I was a plans, operations, intelligence, and patient administration officer, commanding medical companies in the field and working in healthcare staff and administration positions, but having no significant patient contact. I let him know that the iPhone was a tool for research and that with a lack of information from healthcare professionals I had a lot of practice. While there was, of course, lots of medical terminology involved on the Internet, the basic situation was not that complicated. He was a "driver" and said he was glad to know that he could dispense with the elementary background information and get right to the point. That day over a month ago he had told me her condition, CAA, was untreatable and incurable and she would continue to have strokes and I needed to begin thinking now what the "ethical thing to do" was going to be. He all but said she is going to die from this and that I should start making my decisions now as to what her disposition should be. I knew in my heart that I would continue to put her in God's hands. He had this! The doctor and I never discussed it again during her stay in the hospital after her second stroke.

This time, our conversation was even more direct. He woke me from an exhausted sleep and, with her neurologist standing silently by, letting him do all the talking, he said to me, "Mr. Burroughs, we need to talk. I don't think you understand the gravity of the situation." That got me a bit angry but I kept my cool. I reminded him that from our previous conversation a few weeks before I fully understood the gravity of the situation. I was unaware of the reason they had taken her back for another CT scan the night before. No one had said anything to me about it. I was not alarmed, expecting the reading to be much the same as before. He informed me this was different (That was the "gravity of the situation."). The previous night's CT scan, at his direction, had been done with a contrasting agent in order to get a higher resolution image. That CT scan, he said, showed she did not have one new hemorrhage, she had three. The other two were in her right and left frontal lobes. This area affects her reasoning ability—what they call, "executive skills," among other things. He called up the image on the computer to show me. It was plain to see. All this time no one had known the extent of the damage. I have to wonder if it was even there in the frontal lobes when she had her initial CT scan upon admission. At that point he gave me the "ethical" talk again. In essence, I needed to take her home and make her comfortable, and forego any more trips to the hospital for stroke symptoms. Again, there was nothing they could do for her. It would be very unpleasant for her due to all the IVs and interruptions and no rest to speak of. She needed to be kept calm and stress free. I took the message with courage. What choice did I have? There was little to debate. So, again, I punted that message to the Holy Spirit.

When Jan had been admitted four weeks before, she had been assigned a palliative care specialist. This nurse practitioner became a wonderful resource for me. During that admission, she had gotten me a lengthy research paper from the New England Medical Center on Cerebral Amyloid Angiopathy. I read it thoroughly multiple times. She had also shown me Jan's CT image from her second stroke, and took her time with me going over all of that information. Given Jan's CAA diagnosis, this nurse was supposed to help me understand what my options were regarding future care. She knew I had high hopes for a substantive recovery sufficient to get her a lot of aphasia therapy. In retrospect, I don't think she believed that would ever happen, but for my benefit she was supportive and encouraging nonetheless.

During our current admission for her third stroke, I called her again and we began making plans for Jan's discharge. She worked in palliative care, a concept I had never heard of before. My other options were to do nothing special all the way to hospice care. I spoke to a representative from the Visiting Nurse Association (VNA), who would be putting Jan into their Advanced Illness Management (AIM) program if we opted to do palliative care. They also arranged for me to meet a hospice nurse. That meeting started and ended badly. The hospice nurse basically told me Jan would not be on any medications and she would simply be made comfortable. Dying soon was the implication. I turned her down on the spot and said my wife was not dying and she was going to continue being treated for her other medical conditions as before. I went back to the palliative care nurse and the VNA and AIM people and we started making plans. Palliative care made no assumptions other than her condition was a serious "advanced illness." Their objective was to treat Jan at home as much as possible and try to avoid another hospital stay—for any reason, not just a stroke. They had both an internist and a nurse practitioner assigned to Jan and if she needed any lab tests or other diagnostic procedures, they could usually be done at home. They would check on her bi-weekly by phone and a nurse practitioner would meet with her monthly in person. They also wanted to know what medicine she was on, but in no way were they encouraging me to stop giving them to her, though I think the physician assigned to her thought, "What's the point?"

They soon transferred her to the neuro floor to stabilize her further for the next step, which was to take her home.

I had gotten as familiar with the neuro floor as I had been with the neuro ICU. Some of the staff was the same people and they were surprised to see her back so soon. It was clear to me she was merely being cared for until she was ready to safely be discharged. In the meantime, I had a lot of decisions to make. The only unusual complication was another bed sore. They brought in a wound specialist to treat that, but she would still be going home with it unhealed. I frankly think these were preventable. She had one the previous hospital stay as well.

Everything needed to be done at once. I had to get a hospital bed and other durable medical equipment into the house. I had to prepare the house for her return, which included a thorough cleaning and getting rid of a lot of odds and ends. The bed, etc., would be much like what we had when we came home from the hospital and inpatient rehab after the wreck (except an all electric bed). This time, though, there was no end in sight as to how long we would be in that situation. As I was not going to even consider putting her in a nursing home, I had to find home attendants to care for her 24/7. I looked at a few agencies and interviewed a few people who had been recommended to me who had invalid stroke patients at home and had needed the same level of care.

Based upon recommendations, I found a company I wanted to work with. The operations director came to the hospital to meet with me and Jan to determine what I was looking for and to brief me on how they worked. I had a few requirements in staff that I wanted to emphasize and she began to build a team. The next day she came back to the hospital with two in-home attendants and the supervisor. They wanted to meet Jan and me, and I wanted to interview them. Getting the right fit was essential. The cost was astronomical and it had to be as much of what I was looking for as possible. Once we had decided on a team, we arranged the contract and a potential start date.

Our son, Michael, flew to St Louis to help me with these arrangements. John had been in a week before and got a junk collector to take out most of what was in the basement. Michael finished the job. Both were a godsend. For the first time in our marriage, I also hired a maid service to come in and completely clean the entire house (and come back monthly after that). It may seem like an odd thing for me to be wanting, but after the wreck and all the neglect of our place, I really needed to get some order around me. Once that was accomplished it made a huge difference to my mental well-being.

The hospital was willing to delay discharging her for three days until I had all arrangements secured. I really appreciated that. It was another load off my mind.

On July 27th, 2019, we arranged for an ambulance to bring Jan home. The home care team was waiting for her when she arrived. Thus began the chapter we have been on ever since.

Doctors give the facts as they see them, but God is the giver of truth.

Curry Blake

Hospitals are institutions that are built brick by brick on unbelief.

Jeff Randle

Jan in Florence, Italy

Jan and Michael in Florence, Italy

Jan at the Leaning Tower of Pisa, Italy

Michael at the Leaning Tower of Pisa, Italy

Chapter 13

HOME…AGAIN

——————⟋ᰮᰭ⟍——————

AFTER THE WRECK I had cared for Jan at home by myself. With her strokes, I was mentally unprepared for the huge adjustment of having another person in our midst day and night. I had opted to have "live in private duty" support rather than have people working hourly shifts around the clock. For one thing, the cost was less. This was not something that was easily entered into because there are so many things to consider, for example: sleeping, meal preparation, medical material supplying and maintenance, laundry, clothes selection, bathing, dressing, feeding, the care routine (standardizing it), getting used to the different skills and personalities of the care givers, dealing with incontinence, and many other considerations too numerous to mention.

We started with two caregivers who took different parts of the week. Then we added a third so that weekend work could be rotated. One of the first two caregivers, Ophelia, has been with us since the beginning. The second one we also had from the beginning got sick after two months and had to quit. We have had eight people in total pass through our home. Ophelia began working Monday through Wednesday, arriving Monday morning and leaving with a shift change on Thursday morning. She and Jan have a special relationship. There is real love between them and it is a joy (and a relief) to see. She gets the very best out of Jan and is good about engaging her and helping her speak more. They laugh and hug and kiss. Filling that second shift of the week has been a challenge from the start. I have had three other attendants over the months with whom Jan also gets along, but the relationships are not the same as with Ophelia. Some of the other caregivers who have rotated with us have been just short of disastrous. I have gone through seven caregivers in order to fill that shift consistently. Getting a good caregiver to commit for three days including a Saturday, and sustaining that commitment has been difficult. When it has worked out, having only two attendants has been easier for me to manage, and also better for Jan. As I write this we have a good arrangement with only two caregivers.

After several months I asked Ophelia to stay four days per week rather than three and she agreed to do this. It has made a difference for me because of Jan's fondness for her and how therapeutically helpful Ophelia has proven to be for her. I would have Ophelia with us all the time if that were possible, but of course it's not, which is the nature of in-home attendant care. I feel fortunate I have her with us four days each week. When she needs off for any reason it is stressful on us, but of course that happens occasionally. Ophelia is 55 and has been doing this kind of work for over 30 years. Her work ethic is second to none, as is her competence, compassion, attention, and affection for Jan. She has three grown children and is a grandmother. She has had several clients with whom she has worked multiple days for several years. Usually they have been very elderly and in varying degrees of incapacitation. A recent client, with whom she worked for over six years, passed away two weeks before she came to work for us. It is obvious she had a wonderful relationship with that individual and the family. Hearing her talk about that client, and watching her with Jan (and me) lets me know that she would be very content to stay with us for as long as possible. Several times a day she tells Jan how much she loves her. On rare occasion, Jan has surprised Ophelia (and me) and told her she loves her as well.

There has been another down side to our staffing situation. We have a cat, Sasha. I put her in a kennel for boarding following Jan's second stroke. I fully intended to bring her home a month later with Jan. Unfortunately, Ophelia is very allergic to cats and has even been hospitalized due to this allergy. The other caregiver with whom we work is also allergic to cats. Bringing Sasha home has not been an option. My sons and I discussed this. While they were sympathetic, they were correct in their assertion that the focus is on their mother, and the cat situation had to be addressed. The kennel where she is kept has been enormously supportive of our situation and has kept Sasha for eleven months, and has made this more affordable for me. They have known and loved Sasha for years. After several months I had to come to the realization that Sasha must find a new home. Fortunately (God has a way of taking care of even cats.), the kennel has a rescue mission for dogs and cats. They have about 15 cats at any given time, many of which have been signed over to them for various reasons. People know they are a good source to adopt pets. They are well cared for and loved. They can stay there for life if they are not adopted. I arranged with them to have Sasha moved into the rescue section. God willing, she will find another good home and will be loved and doted on as much as she was with Jan and me before her second stroke. I am extremely grateful for these wonderful people. The love they have for pets is palpable.

One of the things we were authorized was home healthcare. We had taken advantage of this when we came home after the wreck. Physical therapy and occupational therapy didn't last very long then, while Jan was non-weight bearing. We had learned how to use the sliding board while in the inpatient rehab hospital, so there was very little we needed to do with physical therapy. It was the speech therapist who took a bit of extra time to ensure she had done as much as could be done to help Jan recover from her head injury. This time, we had physical therapy and occupational therapy (PT and OT) here to help us do passive range of motion exercises needed due to Jan's spastic left leg and arm. We practiced this a few times. The PT also had to ensure that the caregivers are able to transfer Jan from the bed to the wheelchair and back again, which they could easily do. She also tried to get Jan to stand from the bed. Jan had no intention of doing that and objected strongly. "No!" was a word she has had no trouble saying.

I was appreciative of every visit by the OT. She had lots of useful tips for us, especially pertaining to activities of daily living (ADL) for Jan. We worked on having her brush her teeth, feed herself from the table, brush her hair, help with her bathing, help getting herself dressed and undressed. But she needs a lot of assistance.

A nurse practitioner was assigned who checked in on Jan regularly. Like the OT he had the right skills and temperament for his job and I was also grateful for him. He was very encouraging. Jan's vital signs were very good, then, and have remained so.

Speech therapy was another matter. I was very displeased with that. I admit this area was the most urgent for me. I want desperately to converse with Jan again. But her speech therapist only came to the house four times, and then "discharged" Jan because she wasn't making any progress. I had observed her in action. She came with a set of tasks for Jan to perform and as one of them failed, she would move on to the next one and then the next one. There was no therapy per se. None of these tasks were things I would have even remotely expected Jan to be able to do at that point. That did not mean she was unable to respond to speech therapy, as the future was soon to show when I hired her private duty therapist.

I bare the home healthcare speech therapist no malice. What I did object to was the whole home healthcare system itself. Medicare and Tricare pay for this service, but if you get more than four weeks of two times per week therapy, it is the exception rather than the rule. In the case of speech therapy, there was no way anything definitive could have been done in that limited timeframe. On the one hand I can see why they have to respond to what Medicare is willing to pay; on the other hand, I have an intense objection that Medicare does not cover real home healthcare and therapy. The agencies get paid and they build their budgets and income stream on a minimal amount of time with the patient and caregivers, and repeat this process over and over with lots of different patients. With an ever aging population, this industry will continue to have much business under that model. Medicare should provide much more time with patients so that definitive home healthcare can be provided. Not every patient is capable of going to outpatient rehab, which is the case with Jan.

When the speech therapist from the home healthcare agency discharged Jan, I gladly and calmly walked with her to the door. I was pleased that part of the process was over. Now I could move on to real outpatient (home) speech therapy, even if it were at my own expense.

It was during the time when home healthcare was working with us that I reconnected with the private duty speech therapist. She worked part time with private pay patients on Thursdays and Saturdays. I asked her to come on both days as often as she could. Thus began a very good and productive relationship. Ruth is an expert working with aphasia—one of the very best. She has been trained in the US and in Canada. She is a devout Catholic and one of the most patient, caring, loving and knowledgeable healthcare professionals it has been my privilege to know. Her impact on Jan was very effective. I was amazed at how she was able to get

Jan centered and focused on her therapy. I would stay in the room just to watch her work. She was a marvel. She and Jan developed a real love for each other. Jan kissed her often and occasionally told Ruth she loved her. One thing about Ruth I really appreciated was her willingness to treat the care partner like a patient, too. She was always there to answer any question I threw at her, and coach me on a variety of things to do with Jan. She left us with lots of tools we could use on our own time. This relationship went on for several months. Ruth eventually took a full time position. As a result, her being able to continue to work as a private therapist part time won't continue. This was definitely our loss. She is basically irreplaceable.

At first I was fully prepared to pay for her services out of my pocket—and did. One day Ruth surprised me and said that she was now able to bill Medicare and Tricare for her services with us. That took a few weeks to get sorted out, but in the end she saved us a lot of expense by being able to do speech therapy with Jan on an outpatient basis. I helped her a great deal in getting used to working with Medicare and Tricare. Watching her navigate the bureaucracy was continuing education for me on just how laborious the process is for providers to deal with the government as an insurer.

Ruth is a very spiritual Christian. I learned that, like Jan and me, she is an associate of a Catholic religious order. She has more than a passing interest in healing prayer and encouraged me greatly as I grew and developed relationships with divine healers. I have mentioned spiritual gifts earlier in this book, and I will speak to them again in great detail. Ruth is a healer. She has other spiritual gifts as well, e.g., wisdom and faith. I encouraged her to pursue divine healing as another gift she could be applying. Our spiritual connection was every bit as important to me as the great work she did with Jan. Losing her was a great loss.

I gained a better appreciation as to why many providers are not happy dealing with Medicare (aside from the typically lower reimbursement—which was a shock to Ruth). I personally would like to see every person in the US who wants a public healthcare insurance option to be able to purchase it, but my advice to anyone who, God willing, may eventually be able to do this is: Don't expect for it to be an easy system to navigate. The bureaucracy is just too entrenched. I can't count the hours I have spent since our wreck having to keep up with the Medicare and Tricare paperwork. I am able to do it, but I feel sorry for people who don't have the skills or patience to navigate through the process. I endure it because had we not had the coverage from both through the many days of her surgery and other forms of health care, we would have incurred a tremendous amount of debt. Perhaps it would have been less tedious if Jan and I were on a Medicare Advantage Plan, but we opted out of that from the beginning. The experience I had dealing with an advantage plan in the last years of my parents' lives left me not wanting to continue the experience. Despite the administrative hassles, if I had it to do over I would still opt to do the standard Medicare option...and, I'm fortunate to have the military's Tricare system as our secondary provider of insurance.

When we were confined to our home after our wreck, our parish at the time, sent a Eucharistic minister to us each week, which we really appreciated. When we returned to the Church of St. Michael and St George, Jan developed a strong tie in a short amount of time with one of the assistant rectors there, Reverend Tom. Tom is an Anglican priest who moved to the United States from England and can serve here as an Episcopal priest. He served churches in Oxford. Jan did her PhD coursework at Oxford. It is her favorite place in the world. She so likes our church, and likes Tom. He took us under his wing. Since the summer, through two hospital stays and one inpatient rehab experience, Tom was a frequent and faithful visitor, bringing us the Eucharist and performing a healing and anointing liturgy each time. He has continued to visit us at home on a regular basis. I am very grateful for his visits and genuine love for us. He is a welcome respite from my daily activities, and is patient enough to participate in lengthy theological discussions with me during those visits, as I really appreciate the "diversions."

December 17th, 2019, was our 50th wedding anniversary. Before Jan's strokes we had been looking forward to this day very much. Our intention for several years was to renew our wedding vows on that day. When Jan was hospitalized with her strokes I told every healthcare professional we encountered that we must make it to that day. I asked Tom to officiate at our vow renewal ceremony if we made it. There were people who had not been encouraging to me about this happening. There was too much uncertainty, given her condition. I prayed as hard for that day to arrive as I have for anything in recent memory. One physician encouraged me not to wait, saying that we had "known each other" for fifty plus years already and should celebrate that, soon. Only one physician encouraged me. On Jan's last day before coming home I told him our plans and he said, nonchalantly, "That should work." I hung onto those words for dear life! I also had faith enough to believe that it would all work out.

Originally our plan was to have the ceremony at our church and invite lots of friends and our family. As the day approached, it was obvious to me that we would be better served to have the ceremony in our home and still invite some friends and family. I spent about two weeks inviting people who are especially close to us to attend this service. On that day we had 18 people in our house, including family. Tom wrote a special liturgy for us and even ran it by our bishop for input. He put a lot of effort into making this the most special event possible. On that afternoon, Ophelia dressed Jan in a new dress and did her hair and makeup. She looked fabulous and it was obvious that she knew what we were doing, even if she was unable to talk about it. I was happy to the extreme, though, when just before the ceremony started, she held both my hands, looked at me and said clearly, "This is special." and kissed me. I get very emotional even writing about it.

I had our guests bring various food items and take pictures and videos. They outdid themselves. We had a great spread of food and a beautiful cake saying "Happy 50th Anniversary" and with lots of balloons and special napkins and plates.

Seventeen years ago Jan and I made a trip to Hungary and the Czech Republic. While in Hungary, we bought two bottles of a wine for which they are very well known. We made a pact that we would drink one of the bottles on our 50th anniversary and the other on our 60th (Hope springs eternal.). After our guests had left, our son, John, his wife, Shala, Ophelia, Jan and I, opened one of the bottles and shared it around. I toasted our wonderful day, made a short speech about the history of the wine and how much we had looked forward to drinking it, and then we drank. Jan took the first sip and made a face and said, "Yuck!!" At first I was shocked. I thought the wine had gone bad. We all had ours and it was fine. It has been such a long time since Jan has had any wine that I think the sudden taste of it did not appeal to her at all. Normally she likes wine. We all had a good laugh. I still have the other bottle. Heaven knows what it will be like in ten more years. What an absolute blessing it would be if we could share it then...

We have only been out of our house three times in the past nine months; all three were trips to her neurologist, the one she was seeing when she was still able to talk and walk after her first stroke. Back then we were focused on short term memory and cognition loss. The doctor had tested her and it was obvious that Jan had an uphill battle. As I mentioned earlier, she was making good progress when her second stroke hit. Our first visit after coming home was sort of anti-climactic. The doctor had a lot of catching up to do. I had brought along copies of her CT scan reports and a document I prepared outlining the events since May when she had seen her last. At those first meetings following Jan's first stroke, her doctor had put Jan on two memory medications: Memantine and Aricept. I believe, along with the therapy she was receiving, the medicine was helping. At her second visit in December, following her second and third strokes, the doctor was more focused on evaluating her and working toward a future. It was more upbeat, which I appreciated. At the first visit in September, she had done little more than listen, assess, and observe...and catch up on the computer record. After her second visit in December, she noticed some improvement and took note of her patient's progress. I think that was based on Jan's general alertness and her aphasia was not as apparent as before (though far from being healed).

The doctor told me at the end of our December visit that Jan also had dementia. We discussed her encephalopathy from the wreck and the doctor said that Jan's head injury was definitely a contributing factor to her dementia. She also mentioned the 30-plus micro-hemorrhages that had been found on her MRI seven months before, and said those, too, were a contributing dementia factor, as well as the strokes she had suffered. She also mentioned that the beta amyloid protein in her brain (which also severely impacts Alzheimer Disease patients...more on that below) was a contributing factor. The doctor told me Jan's stroke injuries should continue to improve. But she said her dementia would continue to progress. She said, however, that Jan's stroke symptoms would likely improve at a faster rate than her cognition would decline due to her dementia. The doctor wanted to keep Jan on the memory drugs that she had origi-nally prescribed. Fortuitously, those two medications have also been shown to help aphasia patients (as with so much other key informa-tion, I learned on the Internet). The fact that she nonchalantly said she wanted to see Jan again in three months, as though that was an expectation, was a positive sign for me. We had a follow-up visit in three months later at which time the doctor thought Jan was still continuing to improve. She suggested follow up visits every three months. The fourth follow-up visit three months later was done via FaceTime on my iPhone (due to the Coronavirus) which worked out better than I expected. She suggested our next visit be in six months rather than three. I like the fact that her doctor looks to the future.

Ophelia has been with me for the past three doctor's office appointments. Transporting Jan is a challenge as she is unable to help us get her into and out of our car, so Ophelia has to transfer her from the wheelchair to the car and back again.

The doctor said we are doing a great job with Jan and keep doing whatever we are doing. She also emphasized that we take it one day at a time. As I stated before, that is a practice I have mastered.

I had taken Jan to Washington University School of Medicine, to their renowned stroke specialists, about the same time she began seeing her current neurologist after her first stroke. One of those doctors was a memory specialist. He gave Jan an extensive memory test on which she did not perform well. He had seen her scans. He and the stroke specialist she saw there (they were in the same office) suspected Cerebral Amyloid Angiopathy then. It had not been confirmed yet. Even with that assumption the memory specialist made an appointment for her a year in the future and told her he expected she would be doing much better by then. Had her strokes been limited to the first one, I think he would have been correct in his prediction. Short of a miracle (which I expect) her two subsequent strokes have almost ensured that will not be the case.

After her third stroke, I spoke with the stroke specialist at Washington University again and he said what I had heard several times before: CAA is untreatable and incurable and she had a high risk of future strokes. He was very sorry to relay that information to me. He said keep her stress free, keep her blood pressure at or below normal, and avoid any blood thinners (all of which I've done). As I said, I had heard it all before. He suggested I bring her in to see him in about three months. I opted not to do that. Our other neurologist is perfectly capable of following her...and she is more (cautiously) encouraging.

Christmas came and went. I can't remember the last time Jan and I had our two sons and their families in our house at Christmas. Both of our sons came to St. Louis for the occasion, Michael from San Antonio, and John from Denver. We got to spend the entire day and evening together. Ophelia was with us and we all exchanged gifts. Our sons were very generous to Ophelia. She has become family to them. At her mother's house, Michael's wife, Krista, had made lasagna with bread and a salad. It was perfect. We all managed to get around the dining room table and enjoyed ourselves. I was very grateful they had made the effort to be here. Each son had told me that it was very important to be here as they were uncertain about her future. They wanted to have a good Christmas memory in all of this. We achieved that, thanks be to God.

Krista and I discussed Jan's spasticity problem resulting from her last stroke. Krista is a neuro-pediatric physical therapist in San Antonio. She is very knowledgeable about spasticity problems and we discussed an innovative treatment. It was a lengthy discussion about the utilization of Botox for spasticity management, which can be used in conjunction with other treatments to decrease spasticity and improve range of motion. I had heard about a physician in town who specializes in that field. This is something we are pursuing.

I wrote another book in 2011 on the topic of New Leader Integration, written when I was still working as an executive recruiter and coach. I had been contemplating writing a memoir about our experiences when I was a young army officer and we were stationed in Germany. This was a wonderful experience for Jan, Michael and me and while there, almost four years, I had kept a journal. It is a treasure trove of memories of that special time in our lives—some humorous, some tragic, many just basically observational. I have delayed writing that book for many years. Perhaps I will someday. Michael thought it was a better idea to write about what Jan and I have experienced in the past two years, how it has altered our lives, the spiritual journey I have been on, and what I have learned that could be of value to other care partners. I have experienced a lot of what he thought would be useful information and would make a good book for people facing the daunting medical and caregiver problems associated with strokes, and the corresponding spiritual crises some people face. It was hard to argue with that recommendation. Even though this book is also about faith and hope, Krista also said I should not wait for some unseen conclusion, that I had plenty to say at this stage of Jan's recovery. Krista was concerned that I would forget much of what belongs in this book if I continued to delay writing it. And as I write this, (and, hopefully, you, the reader, have made it this far) I hope you have found it to be beneficial as well. There is more useful information to follow. I'm writing entirely from memory. I had made no relevant notes.

I'm assuming that many readers are caregivers of stroke sufferers. If you are a healthcare professional reading this, I hope it is helpful for you to see the full impact of stroke recovery on the caregiver as well as the patient, and what it is like to interact with you. It has been my intent to be direct but fair. Where I have been pleased with our interactions, as you have seen thus far, I have said so. I have also tried not to be petty about things that displeased me while navigating the healthcare system. I hope that has come through as well.

Sister Carla Mae Streeter, OP, who was Jan's academic advisor in graduate school, and dear friend of us both, asked me when Jan suffered her first stroke, and repeatedly for many months, if I was giving her "green matcha tea." Carla Mae is a holistic medicine proponent and I should listen to her more often. At 80+ she is the picture of health and vitality, and extremely sharp of mind. Her spiritual gifts are many, not the least of which are faith, words of knowledge and wisdom. I had mentioned to her that Jan's condition was caused by a toxic beta amyloid protein in the cerebral vessels. When she heard this is when she made the tea recommendation. I deferred. After Jan's second stroke she made the same suggestion. Again I deferred. And after the third stroke I did as well. When I brought Jan home, Carla Mae became more insistent. She said there have been several peer reviewed studies of the positive effects that green matcha tea has on beta amyloid protein plaques. The research began in Japan, primarily working with Alzheimer Disease patients. The beta amyloid protein that affects Jan is the same toxic, plaque-forming protein for Alzheimer Disease that destroys brain tissue. She said if I wanted to continue to be hesitant I should at least do my homework. So I did. While it is anybody's guess whether green matcha tea will improve her condition, Carla Mae convinced me there is certainly no harm in giving it to her. Since August, 2019, Jan gets 12 ounces of the green matcha tea every day. I've shared this story with several people and now have them drinking it as well (including me). In Japan the research suggests it can keep Alzheimer Disease at bay if started early enough. Although the research always confirms that there is no cure for Alzheimer Disease. I'm typically skeptical of all fad claims. But as I said, if it affects beta amyloid protein plaques, what harm can it do?

There is another aspect of this story upon which I will focus for the remainder of the book. That is the spiritual journey we have been on. It has been rich and deeply personal. I have been a faithful person most of my life, and have seen my prayers consistently answered, some amazingly so. But this experience has tested my faith to the brink. I was either going to fall off the edge or I was going to go all in and see where this journey takes us. I am so glad I chose the latter.

Part V

———— ❧ ————

FAITH AND HOPE

Chapter 14

Our Journey of
Faith and Hope

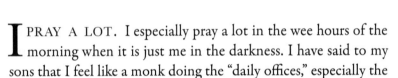

I PRAY A LOT. I especially pray a lot in the wee hours of the morning when it is just me in the darkness. I have said to my sons that I feel like a monk doing the "daily offices," especially the ones they do in the middle of the night. My sleep deprivation also resembles a monk's.

I have been in a heightened state of spiritual awareness since the night of our car crash. Jan and I were able to talk about our experiences up until June 6th 2019 when she could no longer converse with me. I have continued on this journey with her communicating with me in spirit if not usually by voice. I talk to her as though she will always answer me back, but I know that somehow she knows what I am doing and is with me. That is the terrible thing about aphasia. Many people think aphasia patients have lost their intelligence and are oblivious to what is going on around them because they usually don't make much sense when they speak. I don't believe that for a minute! Nor do others who know the facts. Also, countless people who have recovered from aphasia tell the people around them what they were experiencing when still afflicted.

One such vivid account is in the book, *My Stroke of Insight*, by Dr. Jill Bolte Taylor. Dr Taylor suffered a massive hemorrhagic stroke to the left hemisphere of her brain and had severe aphasia (and other of Jan's symptoms) from which, after many years, she recovered. Her book is all about that experience. She also has a fascinating TED talk on the subject available on You Tube. I especially recommend both the book and the TED talk if you are the caregiver of a stroke patient.

Aphasia patients often know what is going on, they just can't interact with any clarity. Fortunately, Ruth, Jan's speech therapist, has reinforced this. As an example, once, when she was working with Jan, she told her that she knew how much Jan loved me and that she must know how much I love her. Jan began to cry and nod her head up and down and looked at me. She appeared very distressed for the first time in her inability to directly converse with me. There was no doubt in my mind, though, that she knew exactly what was being said. Love conquers everything.

While Jan has difficulty making conversation, usually because she has difficulty stringing a sentence together (or, sometimes, more than one sentence together), when her language center is working better, on a few occasions she has held my face in her hands and said, "I love you." When she has been able to voice those words, her face is radiant. Although rare, when it happens, it's a powerful moment for us. This has only happened ten or so times in the past year, but it is the memory of those times that keeps me going—and believing, in her eventual healing. She often pulls me close to her so she can kiss me. As I write this, Jan told her caregiver, Ophelia, that she loves her. I heard it from the other room and went in to check. She was smiling, and also weepy; we believe they were tears of joy.

One day, I felt the need to sit beside Jan and tell her what was going on with her and why. I said she had had two strokes since the first one and she has suffered an inability to speak much and stand or walk. I told her the reason we have 24/7 caregivers is I am unable to give her all the care she needs by myself. I told her we have a legion of people praying for her eventual recovery and that I am sleeping in the den in a recliner every night so she will never be alone. As I went on in this vein she was focused on my face. I only hoped that she understood me, as her aphasia can also block incoming communication. When I finished telling her all of this, I leaned down and kissed her. She looked up at me and said, clearly: "You have done a good job, Michael." It brought tears to my eyes. It still does even to think about this, but it also brings me joy, as I KNOW that God has her by the hand and that he is ensuring that she knows how much she is loved and cared for and has hope. I really needed to hear her say that. I just had no idea how much.

There is nothing I would not do for her. One of the greatest gifts God has given me is to be able to devote so much time and attention to her so that she has absolutely no doubt how much I love her. I know she knows that. While she had receptive language issues following her second stroke and was supposedly unable to understand language directed to her, that didn't last long. Thank God she can often follow what people are saying to her. We find her eavesdropping in on conversations and occasionally interjecting some short yet purposeful comment.

I pray for her all the time. Sometimes I pray over her, anointing her with holy oil. She knows what I am doing. On one occasion she said, "Thank you." She has even crossed herself.

At other times, I say to myself different versions of the "Jesus Prayer." If you are familiar with the Orthodox Christian tradition, they take Paul's exhortation to "pray without ceasing" to heart. There are various forms of this prayer depending on the language; for example, Greek, Russian, English, etc. One English version most talked about is this: "Lord Jesus Christ, Son of God, have mercy on me, a sinner." There are shorter versions, as the prayer is also known as a "breath prayer." It is easier to do continuously if the words flow with one's breathing. I have my own versions of this prayer. They vary, but they are focused on her, mostly, and sometimes on us. "Lord Jesus Christ, have mercy on her." "Lord Jesus Christ, have mercy on us." And sometimes, "Lord Jesus Christ, have mercy on me." I do them during the day, and at night, when all is quiet.

This concluding chapter is about faith and hope. Paul said in Hebrews 11:1 NIV that *Faith is being sure of what we hope for, and certain of what we do not see.* Another biblical term for hope is "confident expectation." So faith is being sure of what we have confidently come to expect with certainty regarding the outcome. Some say that faith and trust are synonymous. I believe that. These two spiritual attributes, faith and hope, are absolutely essential in divine healing prayer which I will discuss more, below.

When we brought Jan home I spent several days wandering around our house looking at everything. Why? Because most of the things in our house remind me of her. Those days were dark for me as I had no idea what tomorrow would bring and I was so afraid there might not be a tomorrow. I found her speaking to me in a quite unexpected way. Although I had not noticed it for a very long time, there is a small framed quote on our dining room wall that says, "Every day is a gift. That's why we call it the *present.*" This is her voice to me. Another message is more direct. Taped to the inside door of one of our cupboards is a green "post it" note on which written by her are the words, "Always believe something wonderful is about to happen." I have no idea when she put it there or why, but it stirs my heart every time I see it now. I'm sure she never imagined when she put it there how very much that note would mean to me in the months ahead. I cherish it. My faith may waiver on occasion, but when I see that note I know in my heart that her faith is my rock.

So even in her current state, I lean on her for confidence and inspiration. The plaque that said "Believe" that had hung on our mantel was moved into the kitchen before her first stroke. It remains there and continues to inspire me. If Jan were able to read I would hope that it would still be an inspiration to her as well.

Is Jesus still healing people today? I grew up in a Christian denomination that assertively preached that the charisms (spiritual gifts) of the Holy Spirit died out with the apostles. (John Calvin had originally asserted this and it was passed down to succeeding protestant denominations over the centuries to the point that this assertion is now assumed to be factual.) As a teenager I knew instinctively this could not be true and met with disfavor from leaders in my church for suggesting so. I never knew at the time where this "cessation" notion came from. While it was always stated as fact, there was never a source to back it up, certainly not a credible biblical one. They also taught that there was no special baptism of the Holy Spirit, today. The assumption had been passed down by generations of the same fundamental and even mainline churches that believed and taught that spiritual gifts had ceased (Calvin's influence). I had more than one member of my denomination tell me that we have the Bible now and "don't need spiritual gifts" to prove that Jesus is the son of God. One need go no further than the early church fathers to refute this (not to mention scripture verses they never quoted to me, such as Acts 19:1-7 and I Corinthians 12 and 14). From the end of the first through the fourth centuries their writings openly talked about everyday Christians performing healing, prophesying, and even casting out demons. Performing those acts then, "signs and wonders," as now, were great forms of evangelism. Jesus told us we would be able to do what he did "and more"...with no planned obsolescence. John Wesley, the famous English cleric and evangelist who led the revival movement in the Church of England recorded over 200 healings in his personal journals.

St. Augustine of Hippo, however, in the fifth century believed that the spiritual gifts had ended because the Church was well established (at least in the Roman Empire) by then and in his view they were no longer necessary (How short sighted he was. I wonder what he would think about an established church in the 21st Century with billions of people living in all corners of the earth, millions of whom are Charismatics.). That is one reason why for centuries the Catholic Church deemphasized spiritual gifts, as Augustine is a venerable influence in Catholicism.

With the Enlightenment, the Catholic Church continued to de-emphasize the spiritual gifts, especially when performed by lay persons. Miracles didn't track well with modernism. In the past fifty years, however, that has changed. In 1967, the Catholic Charismatic Renewal began in earnest. Today there are tens of millions of Catholic Charismatics around the world. The Catholic Church accounts for approximately 1.2 billion Christians in the world today.

In an address in St Peter's Square on June 3, 1998, St John Paul II said, "To all Christians: open yourselves docilely to the gifts of the Spirit! Accept gratefully and obediently the charisms which the Spirit never ceases to bestow on us!" In a separate address to the Catholic Fraternity of Charismatic Covenant Communities and Fellowship, also in June of 1998, he said, "And a survey of the thirty years of history of the Catholic Charismatic Renewal shows that you have helped many people to rediscover the presence and power of the Holy Spirit in their lives, in the life of the Church, and in the life of the world." Pope Francis calls the Charismatic Renewal "a current of grace." He states, "When I think of you Charismatics, the image of the Church herself comes to me, but in a particular way. I think of a great orchestra, where every instrument is different from another and the voices are also different, but all are necessary for the harmony of the music."

There is also a fast growing Pentecostal and Charismatic Church movement occurring around the world, especially in the Global South. Try telling these millions of people that the miracles they are witnessing and performing are figments of their imagination and that there is no baptism of the Holy Spirit. You Tube makes it very easy to witness healings and other miracles.

My focus for the end of this book is on divine healing. Most people give this little thought until something serious happens medically to themselves or a loved one. People put their trust solely in healthcare professionals at times like these, yet there are many physicians who not only believe in the gift of divine healing, they practice it themselves! I know one such physician personally. She is one of the people who has laid hands on Jan for healing in the past before our wreck and her strokes. It has been said that the first place we should turn is in prayer for healing through the Holy Spirit by divine healers and in the name of Jesus, then, if necessary, rely on healthcare professionals to do the work of the Lord with God's hand in control of the outcome. Countless healing miracles have confounded physicians who have made and treated diagnoses that have disappeared through divine healing. These stories abound.

There are other spiritual gifts/charisms. The Apostle Paul, in the book of 1 Corinthians 12:4-11, lists nine gifts of the Holy Spirit, only one of which is healing. He says, *There are different kinds of gifts but the same spirit. There are different kinds of service, but the same Lord. There are different kinds of working, but the same God works all of them in all men."* He says the Christians in Corinth should earnestly desire to receive the "greater" spiritual gifts, but he emphasizes that all spiritual gifts are for the good of the church community and advancing the Kingdom of God. Those nine spiritual gifts are:

- *Utterance of Wisdom*
- *Utterance of Knowledge*

- Faith
- Gifts of Healing
- Working of Miracles (Power)
- Prophecy
- Discernment of Spirits
- Various Kinds of Tongues
- Interpretation of Tongues

"Tongues" in the Bible alternates between known (and unknown) languages at the time, and "tongues of angels." Historically, tongues of angels, often called a prayer language, has also been emphasized, especially as a manifestation of baptism of the Holy Spirit, as in Acts 19:6. Andrew Wommack, one of the most admired preachers and healers in the nation says, "You don't *have* to speak in tongues when you are baptized in the Holy Spirit; you *get* to speak in tongues..." Sister Carla Mae Streeter, OP, shared with me her experience of once attending a charismatic Catholic mass in the football stadium of the University of Notre Dame, where 38,000 Charismatic Catholics were lifting up their voices in praise to God—in tongues. First Corinthians is a letter Paul wrote to the church in Corinth that he established on his missionary journeys. In his letter he gives the Corinthian church lots of instructions in how to live the Christian Life in each others' midst, and uplift and grow the church through the exercising of a collection of spiritual gifts. My point is not to preach a sermon on the currency of spiritual gifts, but to confidently assert for the reader that they are alive and well. In the end, of course, I leave it up to you to believe this or not. I believe it with all my heart. I've seen it work, time and time again. So has Jan.

If you doubt the gift of healing is relevant in the 21ˢᵗ Century, research it. The Catholic Church, during the Second Vatican Council, proclaimed the validity of the spiritual gifts listed by the Apostle Paul in 1 Corinthians 12. There were Catholics already practicing these gifts and had been through the ages, but for centuries they went neglected by Catholic theology and preaching. After the Second Vatican Council the presence and validity of the spiritual gifts was amplified. Within the Church there is a global movement that has been thriving since 1967 called the Catholic Charismatic Renewal. As I have stated, there are now tens of millions of Catholics around the world who have received spiritual gifts through their baptism of the Holy Spirit and put them into practice. Healing is a big part of that movement. Jan and I have not only seen these gifts manifested in our midst, we have personally benefited from them in the past...and helped perform them.

In St Louis, there is a group of charismatic Catholics who meet weekly to praise God and celebrate a charismatic mass. They are called, The Shepherd's Table. Twice a month there is a small cadre of healers who stay behind to minister healing to those who came to the mass for that purpose. Prior to her strokes, Jan and I received ministrations from them on two occasions. In both situations, divine healing or deliverance occurred. We made a public testimony to that affect in their midst. We recently availed ourselves again when, at my request, a healing prayer team of three gifted women with whom we have prayed for ourselves and others several times before, came to our home to lay hands on Jan and pray for her healing. One of these individuals is a physician. I participated in that healing prayer session and laid my hands on Jan, as well.

In 2017, to celebrate the 50th anniversary of the Charismatic Renewal in the Catholic Church, Pope Francis invited charismatic Catholics the world over to convene at the Vatican for a blessing and exhortation to continue in these divine works. Over fifty thousand people from 55 countries attended a mass gathering with him in St. Peter's Square. He admitted that when he was the Archbishop of Argentina in Buenos Aires years ago, Charismatics, and the way they pray (often in tongues) made him uncomfortable. At another gathering that week he knelt while thousands of Charismatics prayed over him in the Roman Olympic Stadium (in tongues). At this gathering, Pope Francis encouraged the crowd saying that they should boldly continue doing what they do, and bring others into the Renewal. He said they are living examples of what the Church should be doing.

The Catholic theologian and seminary professor, Dr. Mary Healy, is also a divine healer. In her work, *Healing: Bringing the Gift of God's Mercy to the World,* she goes into great detail giving examples of divine healing she has either performed or seen performed in the U.S. and abroad, including divine healing performed by physicians. She also lays out a five-step process for healing ministers (i.e., born again Christians) to use. This is not just the work of clergy; most divine healers are lay persons—women and men. In my experience, in the Catholic Church, they have mostly been lay women.

There are many charismatic Christians practicing these gifts who are not Catholics. This movement is growing all around the world under the heading of Pentecostals and the Charismatic Churches. They get this name from the descending of the Holy Spirit on the apostles on the Day of Pentecost (the first baptism of the Holy Spirit). On that day, the promise of Jesus to send to his disciples a helper who would empower them to perform the same miracles as Jesus performed (and more) occurred. This promise extended to the multitude of "believers" who would follow with the spread of Christianity. The debate since the beginning of the Pentecostal movement (in the early 1900's), the Charismatic Church, and the Catholic Charismatic Renewal (1967) is: Are all Christians today empowered in the same way? The belief among charismatic Christians, as taught in the Bible is, yes. It usually follows an act of being baptized in the Holy Spirit, which is different from being baptized with water in the name of Jesus for salvation. This is described in Acts 19: 1-7 NIV. Paul has arrived in Ephesus having left Corinth. *There he finds some disciples and asks them. "Did you receive the Holy*

Spirit when you believed?" They answered, "No, we have not even heard that there is a Holy Spirit." So Paul asked, "Then what baptism did you receive?" "John's baptism," they replied. Paul said, "John's baptism was a baptism of repentance. John told the people to believe in the one coming after him, that is, in Jesus." On hearing this, they were baptized into the name of the Lord Jesus. When Paul placed his hands on them, the Holy Spirit came on them, and they spoke in tongues and prophesied. There were about twelve men in all."

If one wants to see healings and miracles in action, they need to look no further than such people as Curry Blake of Texas, Andrew Wommack of Colorado, or Richard Roberts of Texas, or Jeff Randle of New Hampshire, or Gary Jepsen of Michigan, Pete Cabrera, Jr. of Kansas, or Tony Myers of Virginia, or Jim Holtom of Canada, or Tom Loud of Washington, or Tom Scarrella of Minnisota, or Bob Lindquist and Rick Turner of Illinois and on and on. They go the world over not only healing the sick and injured, but training other Christians to do the same. Curry Blake and Andrew Wommack have trained thousands of Christians around the world to perform divine healing. They teach, and the scriptures bear this out, that every born again Christian has the ability through doubtless, unwavering faith to call for healing of themselves and others through the Holy Spirit that is in them and in the name of Jesus. They have numerous videos on You Tube that make a powerful case for the spiritual gift/charism of healing being alive and well. Another well known healer is Bob Spurlock. Bob is a commercial airline pilot who lives in Alaska and starts churches and performs healing ministry all over the world where his work as a pilot takes him. He has been especially effective in Pakistan and in the Far East.

There is a podcast called, "Heal the Sick," in which the host, Millian Quinteros of Las Vegas, Nevada, regularly interviews a charismatic divine healer from somewhere in the world. His format is to ask the guest to share some examples of healings they have witnessed and performed, then share a bit about their own journey to the point of exercising their gift, and then in the third part, share a lesson that lifts up the listeners. He asks them after each interview to provide the listener with a means to contact them. I have been in contact with several healers through this medium. As I write this, 98 healers have been interviewed, all of whom can be heard in the archives of his podcast.

One thing that is consistently brought out in the media, and in books on the subject, is that the healer is simply a conduit to the healing power of the Holy Spirit that is one with their spirit. While the healer is the instrument of healing, he or she does not do the healing. Healing prayers generally call on the Holy Spirit and command that healing occur in the name of Jesus. There is often not a prayer, per se. Rather, as Jesus and his apostles did, they acknowledge the need for healing and then command that the condition be healed and that the healed person should rise or perform some other action to demonstrate having been healed. They are not commanding God. Empowered by the Holy Spirit within them, they are commanding that a particular infirmity be removed from the person. The essential element is the faith of the healer, not so much the faith of the person who is being healed. There can be no doubt or wavering, whatsoever, on the part of the healer that he or she has the authority and the responsibility to heal people in need. Doubt stops the process. Complete faith in the power to heal, aided by the indwelling of the Holy Spirit, is essential for the healer. Many unbelievers, though, are healed every day.

The churches of the Pentecostal (and charismatic) movement realize that divine healing, as it was in the New Testament, is also a powerful means of evangelism ("signs and wonders"); which is the chief reason why these churches are growing so quickly, especially in the Global South. It is as relevant today as it was on the Day of Pentecost. Millions of people each year are coming to Christ through the miraculous works of the Holy Spirit. These methods are more effective for growing the Church than all other forms of evangelism combined. These healers are easy to find if you search for them. The "Heal the Sick" podcast is a good place to start.

At other times they pray for the subject to be delivered of spirits that inhibit the righteous life or are causing sickness. Doing this is referred to as "deliverance ministry." The book of Mark gives numerous examples of deliverance ministry. This is important for divine healers in that there are situations when the sickness or disease can be directly tied to a harassing spirit of some form. The International Catholic Charismatic Renewal Services Doctrinal Commission even has a book on the subject called, *Deliverance Ministry*. The Church makes a distinction between deliverance and exorcism. Divine healers in the Catholic Church, who are overwhelmingly lay persons, perform a lot of deliverance, they don't do exorcisms. In the Catholic Church only bishops or those appointed by bishops perform exorcisms, which are relatively rare. Pentecostal and Charismatic healers outside of the Catholic Church do not have that restriction.

One of the many guests on the "Heal the Sick" podcast was a healer named Tony Myers, mentioned above. Tony is the author of four books on the subject of divine healing. He is noted around charismatic circles as having gone from being an atheist to being one of the more well-known healers. His journey as a healer began with having prayed himself to divine healing when in desperation he was nearing the end of his life suffering from Lou Gherig's disease. After reading his books, I reached out to him and he has also become a resource to us. Tony points out that some healings occur immediately while others take time. This is a message commonly taught by divine healers. Not every healing is instantaneous. If it doesn't work the first time, come at it again...and again, if necessary. The key is for the healer to begin healing from the position that

Jesus wants us healed and, as with sin, disease and sickness were also nailed to the cross.

After his resurrection and ascension, and on the Day of Pentecost, Jesus ushered in a new era of his kingdom. The Holy Spirit empowers those who have received him to carry on Jesus' mission and grow and edify the Church through the employment of the many gifts of the Holy Spirit (which we are to "eagerly desire," 1 Corinthians 14:1, 12). Before Pentecost Jesus told his disciples not to worry, he would send them the Holy Spirit (helper, counselor) who would empower them to perform the same miracles as he did, and even do more! (John 14:12) I have seen evidence of the power of the Holy Spirit, and all of the gifts, manifested by ordinary Christians who have received or developed certain spiritual gifts/charisms. That there are millions of Charismatics the world over who live every day of their lives in this reality, performing healing and other manifestations of the Holy Spirit, attests to the validity of the claim. The numbers are overwhelming. While it is easy in modern times for many to be highly skeptical of such claims, open your hearts and minds to the reality of this movement. Look around. Do the research. It is happening. It is real. It could make all the difference in the world with respect to your situation.

One well known divine healer, the Irishman, John Gillespie, says that when praying for healing, for oneself or others, we are to "call things into being that are not, as though they were, until they are." Other charismatic writers, Catholics and Protestants alike, point out the need to be persistent in prayer and not to despair if healing does not happen immediately. They say that people doing the praying must believe that Jesus has already healed the person for whom they are praying. What they are praying for is that their infirmities be called out and removed from the body of the person for whom they are praying as they await the manifestations of healing— most of which happen immediately, others take time.

John Gillespie had a deformity of one of his hip joints that got progressively worse as he aged, causing him to have to quit working and remain in a wheelchair. The doctors could do nothing for him. As his condition worsened, he prayed for himself for twelve years, never doubting that he had been healed and that he was simply waiting for his healing to be manifested in God's own time. He was miraculously healed through his own faith and his daily healing prayers and frequent fasting, amazing those who know him. Once this manifestation happened he was told by others that he had the gift of healing and needed to minister healing and deliverance to others. That's all he does today, to great effect. His amazing story is captured in the book, *The Miracle Ship* by Brian O'Hare. Some of his healings take effect immediately, others over time, and still others not at all. John acknowledges that on occasion, no healing takes place. In those cases, he says that God's plan for that person does not include healing. It could also be that the healer was in doubt, wavering, and the healing could not be manifested. God's purpose for us is wholeness, to be free of infirmities, which is why so much divine healing is occurring.

Tony Myers had a similar experience, and once his healing came about, he, too, was called by others with the exhortation that he begin a healing ministry which is all he does today. There are many other examples of people with similar stories who now devote their lives to healing ministry. I should point out that none of the individuals I have mentioned solicit those they have healed for money. They rely on God to provide for their needs when their needs arise—nothing more, nothing less. Most people the world over who perform healings live ordinary lives with ordinary jobs.

Suffice it to say, there are many healing prayers regularly being lifted up for Jan, from many sources who have a long history of healing others through prayer, some of whom have traveled to our home to minister to her. I have asked for signs a few times that her healing is manifesting, and have received them. I strive, however, not to suggest to God a lack of faith on my part by needing signs. Her healing has already happened. Some manifesting signs are there already. God will manifest her healing in his own way in his own time through the Holy Spirit and in the name of Jesus. When I see her healing manifesting, it is always a cause for joy.

One day, I was feeling a deep need to pray "in the Spirit" for Jan. I took a walk around our neighborhood and poured my heart and spirit on Jesus, commanding healing for her in the name of Jesus through the power of the Holy Spirit that I and all Christians baptized in the Holy Spirit have. My challenge was not, "Can I do this?" It was do I have the unwavering faith to do it? This is not something that comes lightly to people. Jesus said that "believers" everywhere are to do it. It was never God's will that people should be sick or diseased. That day I was commanding by the Holy Spirit for her aphasia to be healed. It was the first time I had succeeded in crossing the threshold of some unintentional wavering to complete faith. I prayed for about an hour, repeating the same healing prayer in the manner in which I have been taught—a method that is consistent with all of the divine healers with whom I have consulted and who have also prayed for Jan. When I arrived back at our house I sat on the porch for another half hour and went inside. *Jan greeted me with a conversation,* starting with the words, "Oh, you're home!" as she held out her arms to me. She said that she loved me "so much" (which I had not heard her say since June 6th, 2019, and that she was "very happy" among other things). I would say at this point I was astounded, but I was not. I expected this to happen, which was the difference in my preparation and approach on this day as opposed to other days when apparently I lacked sufficient faith. Her caregiver, Ophelia, was sitting right beside her. She, too, was excited. I enjoyed the brief and loving chat I was having with Jan and was quietly saying "Thank you Jesus" over and over. It was a transcendent moment for us and one I, with the help of other divine healers who are assisting me, am building upon.

"Call things into being that are not, as though they were, until they are." It is a simple formula, but not simple to do the way Christ intended and did himself. He never prayed for God to heal anybody. He simply called for them to rise or be healed in some way or another by the power of the Holy Spirit that resided in him. Before Pentecost his apostles did the same thing—usually in complete faith, except for the example in Matthew 17: 20-21, when they failed and Jesus told them they lacked sufficient faith and, if they had it, they could command a mountain to move "from here to there and it will move. Nothing will be impossible to you."

Once the Apostles were baptized in the Holy Spirit (on the Day of Pentecost) we have no examples in the Bible where their faith was an issue in healing. The healers I have witnessed also do it the same way—unwavering faith, without doubt. On that day I did, too. I now have seen the healing power of the Holy Spirit manifesting in Jan. The Holy Spirit will continue the process of manifesting the healing that has already taken place. We are seeing the beginning of these manifestations as they are making themselves known to us. Other brief conversations have occurred since then.

There are steps to divine healing: Love—Believe (do not doubt)—Expect—Persist (if necessary)—Receive. If you or a loved one is a stroke patient, or is in any other way debilitated, pray about what God has in store for you or that person. It is not difficult to locate Christians who perform divine healing who will come to you in one way or another for that purpose. Or you can go to them. Or if you are a born again Christian, recognize that the Holy Spirit resides in you and with complete, unwavering, doubtless faith, you also have the ability to heal, as you are a "believer."

I have mentioned some of the more well-known healers. There are many more. It's a long list. This Charismatic Renewal is God's plan for the times in which we are living. Christianity is growing as a result of it. Most skeptics who see a verifiable healing actually take place do not remain skeptics for long. Do your homework. If you reach out to them they will do whatever they can do to help you. This is their calling. Divine healing is real. Avail yourself of it. God does not want you or your loved one to have sickness or disease. Scripture says that by Jesus' *...stripes you were healed* (1 Peter 2:24 KJV). Experiencing the power of the Holy Spirit will change your life. This final chapter's treatise on divine healing is a large part of our testimony. Were she not a stroke patient this "discovery" would never have happened.

While I have focused in this chapter on the miracles of divine healing and examples of who practices this and why, we have been blessed by many other people in our lives who have prayed for Jan and continue to do so. Scripture says that, *"...the prayer offered in faith will make the sick person well; the Lord will raise him up...pray for each other so that you may be healed. The prayer of a righteous man is powerful and effective."* James 5: 15-16 NIV I have stopped counting the numbers of people whom I know are praying for her. They come from current people in our circle of friends to old friends to family we haven't seen for decades to numerous people we don't even know. It's amazing! These collective sources of prayer range from each of our high school graduating classes in Nashville, to a community of Catholic Dominican sisters in Racine, Wisconsin, to all of my brothers and sisters around the world in the Anglican Order of Preachers, to the adult Bible class at Long Hollow Baptist Church in Gallatin, Tennessee, to organizations Jan belongs to such as the American Association of University Women (AAUW) to numerous individuals we know are lifting her up daily in prayer. One of these prayers was offered up by her caregiver, Ophelia. I walked into Jan's room one day and Ophelia had just anointed her with holy oil and was praying over her quietly and reverently for healing. That was totally unexpected and it moved me deeply. She prays for her regularly. We are so grateful for the prayer partners that are praying for her from around the nation and the world.

I began this book with words of wisdom that in order to have a testimony one must first have a test. Our test has been laid out in often painful details in this book. It has been difficult for me to relive these difficult times in the writing of it. The beginning of our testimony is the book you are about to finish reading. We hope (confidently expect) a richer testimony in the weeks, months and years ahead of us, or for as long as God wills us the blessing of being together. Our testimony is not dependent on the longevity of either of our lives. It has been our blessing to be married for over fifty years. We have indeed had a blessed life, even in the midst of these tragedies. The happy ending doesn't have to be a Disney movie. We are grateful for the little and big blessings we have already received and we are grateful that we are not making this journey alone. God is with us all of the time. God is good all of the time. And as Paul said to the Philippians: Don't be anxious about anything, pray with confident expectation and thanksgiving about everything, and the peace of God will transcend all understanding through Jesus.

*Always believe something wonderful is about
to happen.*

Jan Burroughs

Jan and Michael Burroughs, Pisa, Italy

EPILOGUE

————⟋◕⟍————

THIS JOURNEY HAS to end somewhere. It has been suggested that as I put a wrap on this book I share with the readers where Jan currently is in this story. As I've already shared, she is being prayed for by believing, gifted people many of whom are divine healers (even from a distance, as the Holy Spirit is not limited by time or space). In short, as I write this, she is improving slowly but steadily. She has been doing so since we brought her home in July, 2019. I attribute this to healing prayer; there is no other explanation. I measure success for the time being in small steps, yet still prayerfully anticipating a leap. The most notable sign of her improvements is her aphasia. She is able to say more purposeful things in an understandable way. She understands a lot of what is being said to her. She smiles a lot. She's very affectionate. She doesn't appear to be in any distress. She is prone to episodes of laughter and glee with me, her caregivers, and visitors. She uses her hands and arms while speaking (for emphasis). She is much better in her ability to focus on those who are interacting with her. She is now able to put weight on her legs to help her caregivers pivot her in the transferring process. She is now able to feed herself from the table and perform other activities of daily living. There are many little things we notice on a daily basis, now. Her vital signs and appetite have remained strong. If she particularly likes a meal she lets you know it. Most importantly, as of this writing, it has been a year since her last stroke, which we were never encouraged by her doctors to expect. She also made it through our 50th Anniversary (five months after we came home) and her 70th birthday, (five months after our anniversary) during that time.

Like John Gillespie who prayed for twelve years for his hip to heal, I am faithful and patient. Her neurologist said to me in two recent visits three months apart that, based on what she was seeing, Jan's strokes will likely continue to improve. She was not saying that after her first visit following her third stroke. She says for us to just keep doing what we're doing. Aside from keeping her calm and as stress free as possible, the only thing we are "doing" is coordinating a deluge of prayers for her healing. The best indicator of her improvement is the reaction I get from friends of ours whose visits are about six to eight weeks apart. Some are stunned at how different she is from their previous visit. It is easy for me to miss some of these changes as I am with her constantly and her improvements are incremental. This is the medical situation. Her improvement is not random or merely ordinary. God's healing power has been at work.

My first book was a professional book written about "onboarding" senior leaders. It was a labor of work. This book is a labor of love. I trust that message has come through. As I write this in mid-2020, I realize there have been some key lessons I have learned, divine and otherwise, over the past two years. As I end this book, here is a good place to share some of them with you.

I coined a term these past two years; I call it, "the tyranny of time." I mention in the book that I had a tendency to live my life in the future and not the present. I have learned we make a huge mistake in life assuming we will continue living normally and life will go on undisturbed, never really changing abnormally, until one day we die. I marvel at how much time I squandered, especially during the three years leading up to our car crash and Jan's strokes. I was consumed with the goings on in our country and world during 2015 through 2017, things over which I had absolutely no control and time which to me, as I've said already, was totally wasted. Millions of others in this country are wasting their lives away doing the same thing when they should drastically rearrange their priorities. This distraction pulled me away from what really mattered most in my life—my day-to-day partnership with the love of my life, Jan.

The thing that caused me pause during that time was a shoulder injury requiring surgery and rehabilitation and the deaths of both of my parents. Losing parents in my late 60s was not an existential crisis. Even though both of them died rather suddenly, their deaths were not totally unexpected and I knew that in the grand scheme of things, they had lived very full and rewarding lives, their times had arrived, and they were ready. I miss them very much.

What I was totally unprepared for was our car crash and the terrible toll it took on our lives throughout 2018. But I instinctively believed that Jan would heal and recover and our lives eventually would happily move on. My instincts were dead wrong. After a very successful recovery from our wreck, Jan having one stroke early in 2019 was a life altering wake-up call for me. It was a blow I knew the after effects of which would remain with us forever. The two strokes that followed over the next five months was my existential crisis. We will never fully recover from this. The best we can hope for is a recovery that will permit us at some point to live out the rest of our days being able to communicate lovingly and in other ways, serve as a testimony to the healing power of the Holy Spirit, and basically function. My prayers for her healing center on that passion and her being spared any more strokes. Any other aspects of healing will be further gifts from God, another cause for rejoicing.

I talk about faith and hope a lot in this book. I have never had my faith tested more in my life as during the past two and a half years. On the other hand, my faith has never been stronger. Paul says in Hebrews 11:1 (NIV) that ...*faith is being sure of what we hope for and certain of what we do not see.* Hope in this sense is not wishful thinking. Biblically, hope is a confident expectation. Faith pulls together what we expect to happen (trust) with what we cannot yet see happening (hope). This is where my focus on healing prayer and other miracles associated with the spiritual gifts laid out by Paul in 1 Corinthians 12 comes from. I have experienced and researched deeply the world of divine healing and associated miracles, and have heard from many people who are authorities on that subject. Before I began the research, Jan and I stepped out in faith on three occasions to benefit (which we did) from having Spirit filled people lay hands on us and pray for serious healing and deliverance needs we shared with them. Our prayers were answered. In my 69 years of life I have occasionally prayed to God for miracles that were answered 100 percent of the time. When I share these with people it simply boggles their minds. Although in a few cases these answered prayers were not what I expected them to be, in every case I was much better off because of those prayers being answered differently from my requests. And I knew that rather quickly. My point here is that in my world, God exists, he is all-caring and all-powerful, and he hears us when we pray to him and will not forsake us. So while our current situation is at the top of a pile of complex prayer requests, God is listening and acting. We have not been put on hold. All I need to do is look and listen, and persist, and trust, and do not doubt. That is where we are as I write this—ever faithful, expectantly hopeful.

I mention in the chapter on Jan's first stroke that I completely missed the signals of her stroke and instead judged it as psychosis. Jan's stroke symptoms were not the traditional ones listed by the Centers for Disease Control and Prevention (CDC) such as 1) trouble seeing, 2) numbness or weakness in the face or limbs, 3) sudden trouble speaking or understanding, 4) sudden and severe headache with no known cause, and 5) sudden dizziness, trouble walking, or loss of balance and coordination. Instead her symptoms came under the heading of "altered mental status." Those symptoms were obvious in her case: 1) disorientation, 2) confusion, 3) sudden behavioral changes, and 4) agitation (other symptoms she did not exhibit until later were unresponsiveness and hallucinating).

The first time, I did not recognize any of those symptoms as being stroke-related. The second and third times I did.

The CDC also reports that 800,000 strokes occur each year in the US. Fifteen percent of those strokes result quickly in death. Each year 140,000 deaths occur from stroke related complications. They also state that one in five American women will have a stroke in their lifetime and 60% of them will eventually die from their stroke. Men are more likely to have a stroke than women, but women are at a higher lifetime risk, attributed to their longer life expectancy. Strokes are the third leading cause of death for women, higher than breast cancer.

I provide these statistics to reemphasize how serious it was that her stroke diagnosis was missed by the staff of the psychiatric hospital that admitted her. I believe her psychiatrist would have noticed this right away, had she been admitted the first day I took her there (when he was still in town). As I previously stated, I kept her from being admitted (reluctantly) at her request. It took her doctor only a few minutes to determine she needed to get to an acute care hospital once he saw her upon his return. I know he would have seen this quickly had he seen her behavior on the hospital floor. Strokes being as common and as life threatening as they are, they need to be ruled out by every intake staff member who evaluates an incoming psychiatric patient. And once she was hospitalized for psychosis, it should not have taken four more days to suspect a neurological problem. She had a house psychiatrist following her and reporting daily to her doctor. He obviously missed it. She could have easily died in that psychiatric hospital as a result of her stroke and not psychosis.

I've also been asked what I learned as a caregiver negotiating the healthcare and insurance system involving severe medical conditions. Here are some of those lessons:

The only way a patient in serious condition can be assured of the best quality of care is if the care partner becomes a fervent patient advocate. Jan and I had several discussions on that topic well before our wreck (She actually felt that patient advocacy might be her calling.) so I was prepared mentally for what I had to do. I have forgotten many situations over the past two and a half years where my having been present, alert, and informed, made all the difference in Jan's well being. Each time I would thank God that she had not been alone and that I was there to watch over her and advocate for her. But even with that level of vigilance, there were two situations where I was only gone for a little while and Jan suffered as a result. Both cases involved the back brace I talk about in our story of the wreck. Had I been there each time, the story would have worked out differently—for the better.

Another lesson from all of this is doctors sometimes have to be assertively stopped in their tracks when the patient advocate has questions. On several occasions I had to insist that I be listened to and that they at least attempt, as best they could, to patiently answer my questions. One physician never had answers for me. I always had to push, and even then, I often did not get answers, not because of my approach, but because the doctor was ill equipped to give me answers. Another doctor asked me if I were a lawyer. I said, "No," and asked why the doctor would suggest that. I heard, "It's because you like to debate." This physician is a kind and caring (if overworked) person. It took all of my will to maintain my composure. I said, simply, that this was no debate, that what I wanted were answers and I had waited a long time for this doctor to be present to answer my questions. Several times that doctor would swoop into Jan's room and spend less than five minutes before swooping out again in a trail of words about how many more patients there were to see, which was undoubtedly true, I'm sure. The last thing that doctor wanted, however, was to be detained by me with more questions. I contrast that physician with the two hospitalists who cared for her following her second stroke. While they, too, were very busy, I got more time with them than I could have ever expected, and let them know how much I appreciated their time and patience, which made a big difference.

The lesson here is that patient advocacy is not for the weak at heart, nor is it for people who do not do their homework and prepare for those brief encounters they will inevitably have with busy physicians. Nor can you always expect physicians to have answers. I found over the past two years for this to especially be the case with stroke patients. I heard more than once that, "We just do not know that much about the brain." While that answer bothers me, it doesn't bother me as much as you might expect. It leaves much room for the Holy Spirit to do his work. I still get answers like that. We got much more definitive feedback from physicians treating her trauma after the wreck, but even in that situation, the encephalopathy she suffered was something for which they could not predict an outcome, as they just didn't know that much about the brain... either. Therapists helped her, but prayer has helped her more. It has been my faith in God that has sustained me. The Holy Spirit understands a lot about the brain...

I mentioned in the book that patients in skilled nursing or long term care facilities are not going to benefit from the same level of competence and care they come to expect in hospitals. This should be no surprise but it is another challenge for care partners. Advocacy and assertiveness are even more critical there. I found the most neglect Jan would encounter as a patient was from some of the staff in that skilled nursing facility. I was frequently engaged in chasing down attendants who were supposedly there to care for her. Our live-in caregivers are CNAs and at one time or another worked in long-term care or skilled nursing facilities. They get irate when they discuss with me what they witnessed while spending time working in those facilities, and they have worked at one time or another in

many of them. Of those who have passed through our home, none
of them were willing to stay in long-term or skilled nursing care,
mainly because it pained them deeply to have to be a party to such
minimal care and negligence on the part of many attendant staff
members. In every case that is why they chose to work as live-in caregivers working one-on-one with invalid patients. They are in complete control of that patient 24/7, and solid, loving relationships
can, and often do, develop. They see, daily, the fruits of their labor.
They don't have to depend on other attendants who can't be found
or whom perform poorly. (I should point out that turnover is high
in these facilities. It is very difficult for them to hire and retain good
attendants, but their staffing models create all sorts of difficulty.) It
is a special calling for the ones who do "live in" care well. If you're in
that situation, and you can, don't settle for less. But even with live
in attendants, you have to screen carefully, establish your standards,
and maintain them.

On many of an occasion I have expressed how deeply grateful I
am that we are both Medicare beneficiaries and that I retired from
the Army and we have Tricare as our supplemental insurance. That
said, I was astounded to have to learn how difficult it can be to wade
through the Medicare bureaucracy. Since we came home from rehab
following our wreck, our dining room table has been covered by
Medicare and Tricare paperwork. It has only gotten more volumi-
nous after three strokes. What I learned was that, despite the tedium
associated with reviewing documents and following up on issues, it
is absolutely essential to budget lots of time to staying on top of it.
In a situation like we have experienced over the past two and a half
years, the consequences of not doing so would be very expensive
and even more frustrating.

The individual who hit us in January of 2018 was not insured.
He also came from a home with very little in the way of supervi-
sion, responsible oversight or assets. He was allowed to run freely

and irresponsibly. His not having car insurance was something I did not fully appreciate until it was too late. He had nothing for which we could lay a claim for bodily injuries. Had we not had Medicare and Tricare, we would have nothing to fall back on for medical care that numbered in the hundreds of thousands of dollars. Our only recourse was our own car insurance, which, admittedly, I had never closely reviewed. Our insurance company is one of the best in the business, yet if I did not carry enough coverage, I could not expect to receive much for personal injuries.

We have a clause called Uninsured Bodily Injury. You likely do as well. We had the minimum amount of coverage for that clause and having substantially more would have cost us very little but would have made a huge difference in the amount of our settlement. Thanks to a very diligent and experienced personal injury attorney, we were able to get the maximum amount possible from our limited personal injury coverage by our insurance company. Had I maxed out on that coverage we would have received triple the amount for personal injuries and damages. It was after the fact I increased the coverage, but the damage was already done.

We are paying down the money we received in that settlement for Jan's in-home care from her strokes. Had I bought more coverage, we would be in much better shape. This has been an expensive and stressful mistake. Look over your car insurance, and where it says Uninsured or Underinsured Bodily Injury, purchase the maximum amount of coverage you can. We never expected to need it. Who does? We were told by several authorities that the numbers of drivers on the road today without liability insurance is staggering. The worse they can suffer is a misdemeanor ticket and suspension of a driver's license. Protect yourself. It's embarrassing for me to have to serve as the poster boy for auto insurance mismanagement.

If you are ever in a situation where you are injured in a car crash (both of us were), find the best possible personal injury attorney you can find. In our case, no one was sued. There was nothing to recover in damages from the person who hit us. Our attorney did not want to pursue it, considering he works on a contingency basis. All of the money, as stated, was recovered from our own insurance policy. Our lawyer at times could be very insistent that we do certain things to help our case move along. Fortunately, I listened to him and tried to do whatever he advised we do thoroughly and in a timely manner. Even with that, Jan's settlement took most of the year. My settlement was not closed until near the end of the following year, which I had to navigate in the midst of Jan's three strokes. These things take time. Mentally prepare for it if you are in that situation. If the uninsured motorist who injured you has assets, don't feel badly about going after some of that in a lawsuit. Your expenses and personal injuries are life altering. Forgiveness is one thing. Do it even if the perpetrator does not seek it, but if it is determined that you could recover more compensation for personal injuries if you were to file a lawsuit, do what it takes to get that. Most likely you will really need it.

Making plans for the end of your life is not something any of us want to do. In our case, we were ill-prepared should we have died in the crash or one of us had died. The strokes are no exception to this. Our son, John, when he came to help out following Jan's second stroke, said that he had learned two things from his visit. Watching me, he said he had learned that love was a "verb" and not just a feeling. He saw love in action and says it has changed his life for the better. The other thing he learned was how important it is to plan for the worst and how little we had done so. He did not know where any of our important papers were (bank deposit box) or how to access this information. He had no idea what our financial situation was. He had no idea whether we had powers of attorney, wills, etc. He did not know where we wanted our funerals to take place or where we wanted to be buried. Neither did our older son,

Michael, have answers to these questions. They often talked about it between themselves. Yes, it is likely that a surviving spouse would have a handle on much of that information, but if both die in the same accident, or the surviving spouse is incapacitated, the situation changes drastically.

One thing I found out I needed was a general power of attorney and a medical power of attorney for Jan (She has one from me, now our sons do.). After her first stroke John tried to urge her to get them for me. I vividly remember the conversation on the speaker phone while sitting on our deck. She, as many people do, felt that there was no rush. She said she wanted to look over her will and determine if it was current, and would do the powers of attorney then. I had serious doubts she would do any of that in her condition. Less than a month from that conversation she had her second stroke and was silenced. There were several important reasons at that point that I needed these powers of attorney. Because I didn't have them, in the midst of all the chaos and angst, I was in the process of obtaining legal guardianship over her, something that requires lots of documentation, a court order and legal fees.

One day, the Holy Spirit told me to go to our bank deposit box to review our documents, something I had already done several times before. I was busy and had no discernible reason to do so, but I went anyway. When I got there, I opened the box and immediately looked in Jan's folder. Her will was there and behind it were the powers of attorney she did for me in 2002! She obviously did not remember doing them, and I had no idea she had ever done them. Having these documents has been vitally important as I care for her and manage her business affairs.

In short, be sure you have all the required personal documentation you need, and ensure that those who need to know have a good understanding of what is in the documentation and where it can be found. Also have all of your financial records in order. When my father passed away (after my mother) he had all of his personal matters well documented and organized in one place and ensured that my sister and I knew where all of that was located. It only took us a few minutes to get what we needed to settle his estate and legal affairs. Since Jan's third stroke I have rectified the situation. Both of our sons are now well-informed and all the necessary documentation is in order. I've gone so far as to make them copies of the most important documents.

Medication is increasingly more important to us as we age. Jan and I take a lot of medications. In each of her hospital and inpatient rehab stays, it was important for the institutions to know all of her medicines. This is an area where we were on top of the need. For years I have had a computer file of all of Jan's medicine as well as my own. We have provided this information to our sons and ensure changes to these medicines are documented. I even have all of her medicine listed on a piece of paper fastened to our refrigerator. I have been asked by lots of people along this care journey what Jan's medicines are. It has made it much simpler for everyone concerned that I am able to print a copy of this at any time—even from my iPhone.

There is a lot one needs to know when serious injury or illness occurs. We never expected to be in this situation. No one ever does.

If you are not in a position as a care partner to a loved one recovering from a stroke you may know someone who is. Consider providing a copy of this book to that person. It has been written to provide hope and encouragement, especially to those individuals.

Hope is not wishful thinking; with faith (trust) it is confident expectation.

Afterword

COVID-19

─────────❧─────────

W HEN I MENTIONED to our family that this book was
finished and ready to send to the publisher, it was suggested
I hold off for a couple of months. The logic was sound; we were in
the early stages of a pandemic and yet the numbers of the sick and
dying became large quickly and they are increasing steadily. How
it ultimately affects us remains to be seen. As I write this, we are
sequestered in our home and have been for a several months. I only
venture out to take a walk or go to the grocery or drug store or ATM
machine or to buy gas (all while wearing a mask). For us it is not
that different than before, as since Jan came home from the hospital
a year ago, I have been with her and our caregivers in our home the
majority of the time. I find things to do besides caring for her and
praying for her healing. For example, this book was birthed in those
circumstances.

Each day tens of thousands of people around the world are
testing positive for the novel coronavirus, COVID-19. We have over
two and a half million known cases now in the U.S. This number
does not reflect those who contracted the virus but were not tested.
Testing (or the lack thereof) remains a major issue. Originally centered in metropolitan areas and counties, recorded cases in rural
parts of America are now occurring at alarming rates.

As of this writing, forty million Americans are out of work and have filed for unemployment (in a four month period) with many more on the horizon. One recent study found that 50 percent more people than were counted filing claims may have qualified for benefits but were stymied in applying or have found the process too difficult. Millions of people around the world are also out of work, while some governments are throwing together unheard of (yet still insufficient) stimulus packages.

Keeping Jan and me from catching this virus is our paramount concern. In her compromised state, she would likely not survive being infected, or me. Hospitals would most likely not treat her in an ICU. She has a living will, as I do. Our caregivers are very conscious of hygiene and sanitation and we wipe down our house with Clorox wipes and Lysol disinfectant frequently. Hand washing and hand sanitizer is the rule of the day. Our best defense is remaining sequestered and managing who can enter our home and ensuring they are wearing a mask. And I wear a mask and gloves whenever I am on an errand, which is the only reason I leave the house. I think long about letting anyone into our home who is not one of Jan's two caregivers, and I've postponed having things done around our house that are not absolutely necessary, just to keep other people away from us for now. Fortunately, both of her caregivers are diligent about hand washing and general in-home sanitation. I'm very confident they are equally as diligent when they are off duty as well. Jan had her most recent neurologist appointment over my iPhone (FaceTime). That actually went better than I expected.

We did have a scare recently when one of our previous caregivers, whose supervisor transported her to our house for her shift, was feared to have been exposed to the virus by her supervisor, who had fallen ill and had to be tested for the virus. Had her supervisor tested positive, that caregiver would have had to be quarantined as would our other caregiver, Ophelia, Jan and I. Fortunately, the supervisor's test was negative, so we dodged that potential crisis. We do not have a "plan B" if we lose our caregivers. The ramifications of which are too numerous to mention. Good caregivers are rare and companies are having a hard time attracting them, especially under virus conditions.

Our son, Michael, and his family are sequestered in San Antonio, Texas. He and his wife are still working out of their house but otherwise staying at home. Our grandson finished his freshman year of college from home, taking his courses on-line. Our granddaughter finished her freshman year of high school, also on-line at home. Our son, John, and his family are sequestered in the Boulder, Colorado region. He and his wife are working from home. Our grandson, there, at four, has enjoyed having his parents with him all day every day. So has their beagle, Kona.

In St. Louis we have all been encouraged to wear masks when out in public due to the belief that the virus can be spread through breathing and not just through coughing or sneezing. Supermarkets and drug stores have installed plexiglass sneeze and cough barriers to protect their check out staff members and pharmacists. There are recorded exhortations played over the intercom in supermarkets urging shoppers to keep their distance from other shoppers. The floors are marked at checkout to ensure that shoppers keep an appropriate distance apart. It's surreal. Drug stores are now encouraging shoppers to rely on the drive-thru for all purchases. Like others around the country, we are to maintain a six feet "social distance" from everyone with whom we come in contact. It will be a long time, if ever, before people shake hands again. People are starting to get used to that. We find clever ways to greet people (from a distance). Waving is one way, as is simply nodding or flashing a "peace sign," etc. A simple "Hello, how are you?" (from a distance) also works. Indoors we can't detect a smiling face, though, due to the masks we are wearing. We're only able to read a person's eyes. That is a strange feeling.

There is debate as to when the virus started in the United States, but one thing that is not in debate is that we were woefully ill prepared for it when COVID-19 hit us with a vengeance in March, 2020. The economy had tanked. The stock market has fluctuated on most days. Everybody has lost something; many have lost much. The unemployed are often people who have lived paycheck to paycheck. The government has attempted to shore up the economy by a massive influx of capital to individuals and to companies. Large companies, such as the airline and cruise line industries, are getting massive bailouts if needed for the good of the country. Small businesses (less than 500 employees) are getting relief also, but that relief is intended to ultimately go to displaced workers with loan forgiveness for their employers if they hire them back. Major retail chains are declaring bankruptcy. It's the "mom and pop" operations that are being left out, but efforts are being made through another round of stimulus to help correct that. As many of these businesses close forever it will change the face of America and affect countless other businesses that support and supply them. There will soon be a glut of commercial real estate possibly more severe than following the financial crisis of 2008—2009. Individuals and couples below a certain income level are receiving some financial relief, though for most of them it is not enough. Unemployment benefit timelines are extended and amounts have increased. We simply at this stage, have no idea just how severe the national and global economic impact of this crisis will be. We can be certain, however, that it will be long lasting—a paradigm shift from the way we were living in this country (and the world) before the pandemic hit us.

States are reeling from the lack of income and sales tax revenue. We also watch how the Federal Government is instituting payroll tax relief and delaying filing income taxes. The payroll tax delay will impact the already underfunded Social Security Trust Fund. We have heard from conservative legislators for decades how we can no longer afford "entitlement programs" such as Social Security and Medicare, yet the government is "creating" trillions of dollars in relief due to the crisis. The old argument that we can no longer afford Social Security or Medicare has lost its credence. These social safety nets will be even more critical in the decades ahead. This virus will redefine how we live and how we care for citizens in dire need of healthcare and financial assistance.

The genie is not yet completely out of the bottle. As this virus progresses, it will be obvious to people who never really paid attention in the past, that it is vitally important that we reengineer our way of life, especially with regard to healthcare and long term care services (Approximately one in five deaths in the U.S. have occurred in long-term care facilities.). We simply have too many people in this country who have no healthcare insurance. Many millions of people are being thrown off of already woefully inadequate healthcare benefits as they lose their jobs. We won't know for many months what the full impact of this situation will be on our society. Without the ability to work, millions more will be stuck with student loans they cannot repay, not to mention the most obvious needs of all—paying rent, buying food and paying for utilities. Nest eggs, for many of those who have them, are disappearing rapidly.

As this is written, we have accounted for two and a half million cases of COVID-19 in the U.S. and 120,000 deaths. In less than four months, according to an Internet search, that is more deaths than we suffered in every war the US has fought in since the Korean War began in 1950 (100,818). Future prediction models are based on how soon state governors will open up businesses and other gathering places for individuals. This is starting to happen with some restrictions remaining in place. The more lax the restrictions are, the greater the risk to the population. Health organizations making ever increasing projections are not swayed by government optimism associated with getting the country back to business state-by-state.

It remains an inevitable prediction that in the fall and winter (2020-2021) we will see a resurgence of the virus because it is so transmissible and it has globally spread. If another round hits us then it will coincide with flu season. During the 2019-2020 flu season there were at least 39 million cases of flu resulting in 24,000 deaths—and that is with a virus that has a vaccination available. Having a COVID-19 resurgence on top of flu season could create a lot of confusion because of the overlap in symptoms. Often the second wave of a pandemic is worse than the first wave. This was the case with the Spanish Flu in 1918. The more lethal second wave hit the country in September after a much milder winter and spring. The Center for Infectious Disease and Research Policy (CIDRAP) predicts that the Covid-19 pandemic is not going to stop until it infects 60 to 70 percent of people.

With all that said, our Missouri governor has decreed that every business throughout the state can reopen under what he calls his "gradual" and "strategic" reopening plan. Social distancing will still be a top priority. There are, however, no longer any restrictions on social gatherings. There will also be occupancy limits, although it is uncertain as to how to enforce them. It will be fewer orders at this point from the state's administration and be more consumer-driven. The order will be reevaluated at a future date, but it is hard to imagine that people would willingly sequester again (or businesses close) now that they are moving about freely again.

Unless I were to create a running journal of the daily crisis we are living through, there is no point in trying to relate all this evolving virus-related global pain and anguish to Jan's stroke situation and our quest for her healing. They are separate and distinct. There is also no information yet evolving on the part of the healing ministries with which we are in contact as to how this virus is impacting them and how they are ministering to their fellow men and women who have healing needs or who have contracted the virus. It varies. What I have been able to discern, however, is that a few of them are healing the sick in the usual way where physical contact is normal. Some ministries continue by phone. Others are even going on-line to use scripture as a basis for encouraging people to not be afraid and to have faith. Several of them have based their encouragement on Psalm 91 NIV (*He who dwells in the shelter of the Most High will rest in the shadow of the Almighty...Surely he will save you from the deadly pestilence. You will not fear the terror of the night...nor the pestilence that stalks the darkness, nor the plague that destroys at midday. A thousand may fall at your side, ten thousand at your right hand, but it will not come near you. If you make the Most High your dwelling...then no harm will befall you, no disaster will come near your tent. For he will command his angels concerning you to guard you in all your ways...*)

As we have been told to keep a "social distance" from people, it's harder to lay hands on the sick from six feet away (But the laying on of hands is not essential for healing, anyway. The Holy Spirit is not limited by time or space.). Healing can, and does, often occur by phone or even text message. Many well-known healers have refused to let the virus curtail how they perform their healing ministries. Suffice it to say, that the need for divine healing (and healers) has shifted into overdrive. It also remains to be seen if this global crisis will cause a resurgence of religious belief. It's hard to predict given how (as of this writing) the majority of churches have shut their doors for now and their services are being held virtually via live streaming. In some states, restrictions on assembling for religious services are beginning to ease. Many people object to these restrictions, anyway, saying it infringes upon their Constitutional rights. This has been a hot political topic.

It's early in the crisis. In addition to practicing social distancing, we have been told to "shelter in place." This is easing in several states.

This is the closest thing to a global apocalypse as most people alive today have ever imagined. Others merely see this crisis as a gross inconvenience.

Families are now separated in ways that were never thought to be a problem before this crisis. In our widely distributed society, how many elderly parents, many of whom are medically compromised, are now separated for who knows how long from their adult sons and daughters (as we are)? How many situations are on the horizon where these people will have seen their parents and grandparents for the last time? I am glad my own parents who died the year before our wreck, did not have to live their final years in this "new normal." Before, I was just glad that through our wreck and Jan's strokes they did not have to suffer helplessly with us from hundreds of miles away (being unable to travel to help us). If they were alive today and caught the virus, in Jan's present condition we would not be able to help them, and vice versa.

This virus has had a significant impact on my psyche. Over the past two years I have often said that with our wreck and her strokes, Jan and I were deprived of an enjoyable and comfortable retirement that we had always saved for and anticipated. The wreck was a cause for frustration as we had plans to frequently visit our sons and their families in Texas and Colorado, other family members in Tennessee, and to travel back to Europe, especially Germany (where we lived for almost four years and have not returned since leaving in 1976) and to visit places we had not yet been. In addition to her strokes, this pandemic has demonstrated yet again how futile those dreams were. Even if Jan were never to have been broken so badly in our wreck, or reduced to an invalid state through her strokes, we would be unable to travel any more in this way. It will be a long time before Americans, en masse, will take overseas vacations or routinely fly around the country on overly crowded airplanes. But still, by the grace of God, I feel paradoxically blessed rather than robbed. We have had a great life. Should we survive, and Jan be healed sufficiently, our next phase will be ministry and sharing our testimony, not globetrotting. I won't have to travel far; the ministry field is vast and full of need and opportunity in St. Louis where we live.

The impact of this pandemic will remain with Jan and me for the remainder of our lives. But as this book goes to print, there has been a need for me to address this situation in light of our medical and faith journey. Until four months ago, we had a mountain to move in our lives—her stroke recovery, and faith and hope prevailed via our immersion into the world of divine healing. We remain focused on her healing, and pray that with prudent measures on our part, and patience, we will be spared from this virus. And we pray our family will be spared in the same way.

This book is called, *Moving Mountains: Facing Strokes with Faith and Hope.* I have gone to great lengths to share how we are moving with faith and hope through Jan's stroke recovery. In this Afterword I have not spoken much about faith and hope. I've laid out the grim reality of this pandemic as it unfolds. That said, in our world, nothing is too big for the Holy Spirit. If we are able to face each day of Jan's stroke recovery with hope (i.e., confident expectation) then it would show a profound lack of faith and hope for us to view this pandemic as a different threat to us. Both her strokes and the potential for a virus infection are real situations, true, but we face other risks every day of our lives. Our faith in God is complete. We simply can't live each day in fear of death from the virus or any other cause. What is absolutely essential for true believers is to live through this pandemic one day at a time, for that's all we have, really, and not succumb to fear and anxiety. *Do not be anxious about anything, but in everything by prayer and petition, with thanksgiving, present your requests to God, and the peace of God, which transcends all understanding, will guard your hearts and your minds in Christ Jesus.* Philippians 4: 6,7 NIV

Many people are genuinely afraid. The greatest commandment is that I am to love God with all my heart, soul, mind and strength, and love my neighbor as myself, Mark 12:30. Not taking the standard precautions would show a lack of love for my neighbor.

No Man is an Island (John Donne).

I'll continue to do what Sister Carla Mae encouraged me to do months ago: Thank God each night for at least three things that transpired during the day just ending. My prayer is like a song put on repeat play. I start by thanking God for his unfathomable love and for walking this stroke recovery journey with us and helping us, through the power of the Holy Spirit, and in the name of Jesus, to mark our progress with little miracles that are occurring routinely as we wait faithfully for bigger miracles. I then thank God for Jan and me having made it through another day—again, one day at a time. This pandemic does not really change that practice for me; I just add another element to my prayer of thanksgiving, that we made it through another day of this pandemic as well, and that our sons and their families have done the same. All we have is today. We must make each day count to the fullest, with both its blessings and its challenges. James 4:14 NIV says: *What is your life? You are a mist that appears for a little while and then vanishes.* This is all the more reason why we must make each day count, love one another, and trust God completely.

Our world has forever and drastically changed. It will continue to do so. Plagues and pandemics have been happening for millennia. We have much on which to focus for the remainder of our lives. I'm still on the quest for Jan's recovery as more and more divine healers graciously enter our sphere, which will continue for as long as we live and breathe.

Faith is the victory that overcomes the world.

ABOUT THE AUTHOR

————⚬⟨⟩⚬————

MICHAEL K. BURROUGHS is a lay religious brother of the Anglican Order of Preachers (Dominican) and an Associate of the Dominican Sisters of Racine, Wisconsin. He is a graduate and former mentor and diocesan coordinator for the Education for Ministry program through the School of Theology at the University of the South (Sewanee). He was baptized in the Holy Spirit when he was twenty and has only in later life begun to rekindle his spiritual gifts. Michael is a retired U.S. Army colonel, a former global executive recruiter and leadership coach, and is the author of *Before Onboarding: How to Integrate New Leaders for Quick and Sustained Results (2011)*.

For healing ministry or to otherwise contact Michael, email him at: AgoraMinister@gmail.com

CPSIA information can be obtained
at www.ICGtesting.com
Printed in the USA
BVHW090849040522
635996BV00045B/4246